Ready-to-Go Scripture Skits

(That Teach Serious Stuff)

The Sequel

For Christopher Michael Theisen,
a gentle soul, a listening ear.
May your becoming soon enlighten the world
as your presence has enlightened mine
for the past twenty years.

And with thankfulness and love to my wife, Mary,
and children, Chris, David, and Rachel,
for the time you give me to act up.

Ready-to-Go Scripture Skits

(That Teach Serious Stuff)

The Sequel

Michael Theisen

Saint Mary's Press®

Genuine recycled paper with 10% post-consumer waste. 5108300

The publishing team included Laurie Delgatto, development editor; Lorraine Kilmartin, reviewer; C. J. Potter, illustrator and cover designer; prepress and manufacturing coordinated by the prepublication and production services departments of Saint Mary's Press.

Printed in the United States of America

Printing: 9 8 7 6 5 4 3 2 1

Year: 2013 12 11 10 09 08 07 06 05

ISBN 0-88489-896-2

Library of Congress Cataloging-in-Publication Data

Theisen, Michael.
    Ready-to-go Scripture skits (that teach serious stuff) : the sequel / Michael Theisen.
        p. cm.
ISBN 0-88489-896-2 (spiral)
        1. Drama in Christian education. 2. Bible plays, American. I. Title.
BV1534.4.T45 2005
268'.433—dc22

                                                                                    2005005100

Contents

The Laborers in the Vineyard

The Rich Man and Lazarus

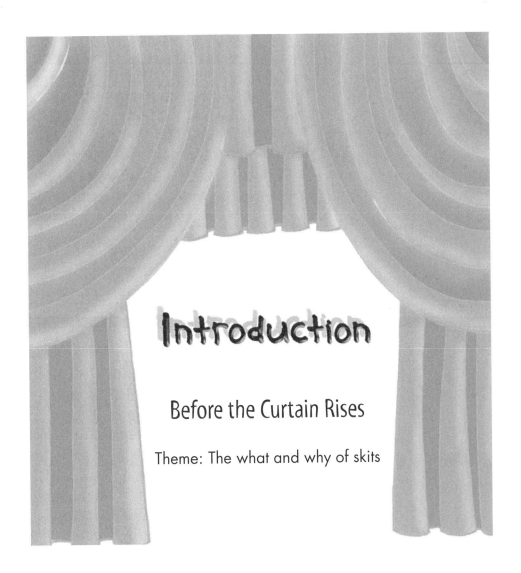

Introduction

Before the Curtain Rises

Theme: The what and why of skits

Are You Ready for a Completely Different Way of Teaching?

Welcome back to *Ready-to-Go Scripture Skits (That Teach Serious Stuff)—The Sequel,* the book that will help you to engage young people in examining and exploring the Scriptures in a way that will have parents and neighbors wondering, "Is it legal to have so much fun at church?" The answer, of course, is absolutely, positively, *we hope so.*

By now you are probably wondering, along with those suspicious neighbors and quizzical parents: *Why skits?* Don't our young people act up enough already?

Let's answer that question with a little memory test:

1. Do you remember reading your high school text on Church history?
2. Do you remember the lecture on the synoptic Gospels?

3. How about the seven deadly sins?
4. The corporal works of mercy?
5. The Ninety-five Theses?
6. What did you get from your true love on the eleventh day of Christmas?

Now see how you do in answering these questions:

1. Would you characterize your first role in a play as that of an animal, a vegetable, or a mineral?
2. Can you still recall the one line you were assigned in the fifth-grade production?
3. Do you secretly crave reliving those silly retreat and camp skits, even as an adult?

If you are like most people . . . uh, scratch that, because if you *were* like most people, you'd be playing golf or taking a nap instead of reading this intro. The point is, people remember and recall what they *experience* much more easily than what they are told or what they read. If you doubt that, spend five minutes listening to any teenager in the universe talk about what he or she remembers from two years ago. Most likely it's *not* going to fit under the category "All-Time Favorite Lecture" or "The Textbook I Continue to Read Each Night." Experience-based learning is a technique we learning theorists refer to as active learning, and for many reasons, it works with young people (it actually works with old people too, but they don't readily admit that).

The fact that you can remember your starring role in your second-grade Christmas pageant—and that you forgot all your lines after tripping and falling on the way to the manger—has a lot to do with the fact that you were actively engaged in that experience. Even though you continue to confuse "starring role" with actually portraying "a star," that shining moment is still perched at the top of your memory list, outplacing chapter six of your Church history text. To a large extent, that is because drama uses just about all your senses and puts you "out there," taking a risk onstage, entertaining a crowd, and possibly even teaching a lesson (insert "gasp!" here).

To put it simply, *Ready-to-Go Scripture Skits* engages the participants in an active form of learning that is hard to beat. It achieves MLP (maximum learning potential) through FLP (full laugh potential). Plus the skits are so off-the-wall that you will have no problem involving just about everybody in your group one way or another (actually most of the participants will have no choice in the matter!). Best of all, the Ready-to-Go

Scripture Skits are just that: ready-to-go. Few props are used, no lines need to be memorized, and you do not have to worry about the special lighting effects blowing the circuit breaker. In fact, producing them is the closest you'll come to that memorable experience of your second-grade Christmas pageant—only this time, you will be instructing people to fall down!

Behind the Scenes:
The Three E's of Learning

There are three acts, or movements, to each session in *Ready-to-Go Scripture Skits—The Sequel*. Each act is part of a continuous learning process designed to take the audience to a deeper level, until, by the end of act 3, they are completely hypnotized and under your total control. Before you wake them from that hypnotic state, I recommend that you inform each of them of a different gift you'd like to receive next Christmas. And while you are contemplating that Christmas list, read on to find out a little more about the three E's that make up each session.

Most moments of learning start here, at the point of engaging the learner. Unfortunately many end here as well because we dismiss some of the more creative ideas that grab young people's attention these days, like bungee jumping and Splatball. Act 1 is all about grabbing their attention and holding on to it, but unlike those over-the-top methods, it does not risk their lives (their reputations might be another matter).

Each session begins with the director (a.k.a.: you) asking for volunteers from the audience (a.k.a.: them), which quickly moves into the director grabbing volunteers from the audience and assigning them the various roles called for in the Scripture skit. The director then tells the actors to wait offstage until their parts are announced, which is just a nice way of telling them to get out of the way until they are needed. Next the director (a.k.a.: the one smart enough to be reading the script rather than acting it out) instructs the actors *and* the audience members that each must do *exactly what is read, when it is read.* The director will know when someone is supposed to act because in the script, the action statements are followed by ellipsis points (a.k.a.: three dots that look like this: . . .).

Whenever there are ellipsis points, the director pauses—and in some cases needs to repeat the action statement . . . and in some cases needs to repeat the action statement—to signal that the action must be performed before the show can go on. For example, the director might read, "They froze in their tracks . . . ," and while pausing notice that the actors are still moving. In that case, the director might need to say again, loudly, *"I said, 'FROZE in their tracks . . . ,'"* while giving them the evil director's eye that literally does freeze them in their tracks.

Because each Scripture skit is a bit different from the biblical story most of us hear at church (okay, okay, *a lot* different), it will not only *keep* the actors paying attention, it will *require* them to pay attention in order to keep up with what is going on and what is being asked of them. The same holds true for the unsuspecting audience members who mistakenly think they are safe because they are not onstage *[insert diabolical laugh here].* The director knows that *no one is safe* from a Scripture skit, especially the audience. That is because many of the skits require the audience to be fully, consciously, and actively involved and on their best behavior, ready to be called on at any moment to do something really important (kind of like being in church on Sunday!).

Another feature of the Scripture skits is the cue card. This is a set of lines that a specific actor must say out loud, usually in the voice of someone else, such as a famous actor or cartoon character. You might find it helpful, while twisting someone's arm to volunteer for a cue card role, to make sure that the person is able and willing to speak in the required voice. On the other hand, it can be really funny to watch a junior high girl discover at the last second that she must speak like Darth Vader. No matter which strategy you choose for maintaining your FLP, when it comes time for a cue card, simply hold the book in front of the actor who must read it and point to the box that the lines appear in. Because these Scripture skits are ready-to-go, they give no time for line memorization or character development—it's improv or bust! The point of act 1 is to grab the attention of the audience and of the actors.

The point of act 2 is to help them continue their star trek, leading them to new frontiers, where no one has gone before. All bad *Star Trek* metaphors aside, the real point is to take them to another level of insight regarding the Scripture story they just acted out and its application for life today.

First the audience is asked to hear the story one more time, as it actually appears in the Scriptures. I suggest that, if possible, you use the New American Bible translation because it's the one we hear proclaimed at Mass. It's always a good idea to have a young person read the passage, and it's an even better idea to make sure that that person *can* read it (as well as pronounce all the words in it). So when you first gather the group together, even before recruiting your actors, recruit someone to do the Scripture reading during act 2, and give that person a Bible with the reading marked, to look over while you recruit the actors. That will do two things: it will give the young person time to familiarize himself or herself with the reading, and it will give you a free hand for holding the *Ready-to-Go Scripture Skits* book!

After the proclamation of the reading, a series of commentaries give some important background and insights into the historical origins of the story as well as its meaning for us today. This is the part of the session where the robot from *Lost in Space* would yell mechanically: *"Danger, Will Robinson. Danger."* Why? Because you may be tempted to begin lecturing your audience back to la-la land. To avoid falling into that old trap, try to spice up these important points a little by *keeping your audience involved.* Each commentary is designed as a little "byte" that is easily swallowed. Each "byte" is highlighted with a boldfaced subhead. You are strongly encouraged to type or write each of those boldfaced subheads on a separate 8½-by-11-inch sheet of paper and hand the sheets to various actors to hold up for the audience as you briefly describe the commentaries that go with them.

That will accomplish three things: First it will make you appear really well prepared and smart—and, let's face it, when was the last time someone accused you of being that? Second it will keep the audience involved and offer them a visual image highlighting what you are talking about, thereby increasing the MLP (maximum learning potential) of all those within a 3-mile radius of where you stand. Finally it will provide the entire group with the ideal opportunity to make helpful mental notes that they can refer back to when they go exploring in act 3.

Act 3 brings the audience back to life—theirs! Its purpose is to help them relate the Scripture story and its themes to their lives today. That will enable them to appropriate the meaning of the Scripture story so that they can discover, as Dr. Frankenstein did after creating his monster, that "it's alive!" For that to happen, the director must help the young people make sense of the powerful story that is unfolding before them. Act 3 provides two phases, or scenes, that you can use to achieve that goal.

The first scene, called "Reflection and Discussion," usually involves a breakup or two, or three. That is, the large group breaks up into pairs or, most often, small groups of four to six people. This small-group dynamic is designed to offer everyone an opportunity to actively explore and discuss what they have heard and experienced, in order to reflect on what it means for their lives and the world today.

The second scene, or phase, to act 3 is the "Curtain Call." This is when the entire group gathers back together to share their thoughts and ideas about the three acts and the themes that were touched on and what the Scripture passage may be asking of young people today. Each curtain call ends with a moment of reflection and prayer. During this time, it might be a good idea to play some reflective music or a popular song that speaks to the themes covered in the session. Not only can reflective music help the young people to focus internally on what God may be asking of them, but it could help you to justify purchasing that new CD player you've been eyeing.

A General Warning

The Scripture General has warned that Ready-to-Go products may be harmful to your mental health. Please do not use this book while operating heavy machinery or if you lack a sense of humor. Consistent users are strongly encouraged to take frequent breaks from these skits in order to discover the other half of the secret of life. If you find yourself constantly thinking of new and tricky ways you can use these skits at staff luncheons or at the family dinner table, then please seek professional help immediately—in the form of an acting career.

Here are some other reminders and warnings that you might find helpful as you sink deeper and deeper into the delightfully dangerous world of *Ready-to-Go Scripture Skits—The Sequel:*

There are three acts for a reason. It might be tempting to enjoy the laughter of a Scripture skit and then pull the curtain closed after act 1. Don't give in to that temptation (Jesus didn't!). The Scripture skits are means to an end, and laughs are not that end. The process is designed to spiral inward, so that each act takes the learner to a deeper, more meaningful level. Most sessions, if all three acts are done, will take 60 to 75 minutes to complete, depending on group size. If you must cut out a section owing to time constraints, cut out the activity portion of act 3 and go immediately to the curtain call. You can also change or skip some of the curtain call questions to suit your group, but please be faithful to concluding each session in prayer and sharing.

Stop and smell the roses. Which is simply an elegant way of saying, "Take . . . your . . . time . . . ," while reading the skit in act 1. Be sure to pause for the action (and laughs) to unfold, so that you can reach that coveted FLP (full laugh potential). The best way to do that is to read the skit to yourself out loud (and out of earshot of curious neighbors) *before* using it with a live, and potentially unpredictable, audience. That will give you time to get a feel for the action movements and where and when the really funny parts occur. It will also give you time and space to see if any quick script changes need to be made owing to your group's age or size, whether members have taken a bath lately, what they've eaten right before the skit, or other special concerns.

Don't forget to KISS. That's right, KISS (keep it short, silly). This is especially true when you are in the middle of act 2, examining the meaning of the Scripture reading. Make your mantra the same as that of the casting director for the Munchkins in *The Wizard of Oz:* "The shorter, the better." Trust that the participants will get the point if you keep that point short and sharp.

It's the action, not the actor. The ham. Every group has at least one, and you'll find out who they are in your group soon after you start using these Scripture skits. Hams love to hog the stage—but offering them opportunities to do so is not the purpose of *Ready-to-Go Scripture Skits.* The point is not to see who can become the best actor, but to engage as many people as possible in telling and understanding the Scriptures. This means that the hams in your group should not be selected for the leading roles every time, even though they are the ones who will arrive early . . . with gifts of chocolate . . . when they sense a Scripture skit coming on. To avoid favoritism and give everyone an equal chance to be onstage, you may want to put every person's name into a box, then call out a Scripture skit role and randomly pull a name from the box.

Forget the gender. Unfortunately women are not represented as frequently as men in many of the Scripture stories, so there are more roles for men. In the words of my eight-year-old daughter, "IT ISN'T FAIR!" And frankly, she's right, so ignore the gender. If Shakespeare could have his male actors play female characters, then, by golly, why can't the director of these skits have female actors play male roles? Don't worry if a woman is chosen to play the man born blind or a guy is cast as Moses's sister, Miriam. Some of the best laughs might just occur when the gender roles are purposely switched or drawn at random.

Learn to just say no. *No* is not a word that we like to use, but it's better if we begin to face the hard truth now: *No,* we can't act up every moment of every day. Your young people are going to love doing Scripture skits, and you'll become addicted to their screams and cheers to learn more about the Scriptures. At some point, however, you are going to have to convey to the young people that there is more to life than acts 1, 2, and 3. When you reach that point, tell them it's time to stop acting up and start playing (and then introduce them to *Ready-to-Go Game Shows!*).

Create your own. Once you have the gist of all this, why not get really creative and assign some other Scripture stories to small groups and lead them in creating their own Ready-to-Go Scripture skits? While some small groups are writing the scripts, have others use Bible commentaries to look up and summarize the important points of the Scripture story, creating a few questions that will invite the whole group to reflect on how the story applies to their lives. Then take turns presenting the skits to the large group over the course of several weeks. Not only will your young people learn 3 trillion percent more this way, you may just inspire someone to become the Cecil B. DeMille of the twenty-first century!

Consider the Possibilities

There are ten sessions in *Ready-to-Go Scripture Skits—The Sequel,* each highlighting a different Scripture story and focusing on one or more themes that you can connect with young people's lives today. Besides using these Scripture skits as sessions unto themselves, think about using them in one or more of the following settings:

Retreats and lock-ins. What's a retreat without an opportunity to act out? Use *Ready-to-Go Scripture Skits—The Sequel* as a creative way to spice up your next retreat or lock-in, and as a strategy for introducing a talk or activity on a theme such as forgiveness, the power of God, or Gospel justice.

Prayer services. If you want to really pray the message of the reading, use acts 1 and 2 of a Scripture skit to get the group's attention and focus it on the meaning of the Scripture passage. That way, you've got the reading and the sermon all rolled up in a user-friendly experience that will focus the young people powerfully and attentively on prayer.

Parent-teen events. Want to get put on your teens' electronic buddy lists? Then make their parents star in a Ready-to-Go Scripture skit! These serve as terrific generation breakers, allowing youth and adults alike to laugh and learn at the same time. There's nothing that breaks down those generational walls quicker than giving teens the chance to watch a parent impersonate Zacchaeus as a Munchkin or to be asked to play one of the dancing vineyard workers in the parable of the laborers in the vineyard.

Catechist and volunteer training. The best way to show those who teach our young people another way to teach is to, well . . . *show them!* Why not begin your next training session or youth advisory board meeting with one of these skits, and give your youth ministry leaders a firsthand experience of how learning is not only fun but an outrageous act of faith!

The Exodus—Part 1: The Ten Plagues

Produced by
Exodus, Chapters 3–14

Themes: Covenant
and call, power of God

Synopsis

This Scripture story examines the developing relationship between Moses and Yahweh, so that the audience may begin to see how God is made visible and present in their lives, and to discover how God is calling each of them into a relationship.

Props

☐ a staff (This could be any stick, broom, or mop that is handy.)

Cast (4 people plus the entire audience)

☐ voice of God (spoken loudly through cupped hands as if shouting from far away)
☐ Moses (must know the tune to "Pharaoh, Pharaoh" a.k.a.: "Louie, Louie")
☐ Aaron (speaks like Bugs Bunny), holds the staff
☐ Pharaoh (speaks like Elmer Fudd)
☐ the audience

If this is the first skit the group has done . . .
Explain that the characters selected are to do *exactly* what they hear the director read and are to be sure to face the audience during the performance. You should pause at each ellipsis (. . .) to give the characters time to do what you just read. When you come across a cue card, hold the book in front of the character who must read it, and point to the box containing the lines while emphasizing the voice in which it is to be read. Take your time and let the laughs roll!

During the skit, the audience will be instructed to do various things, which they should do when they hear it announced in the script. Give the staff to Aaron to hold before beginning the skit.

Skit

One day Moses was sitting down warming his bare feet . . . by the fire of a burning bush . . . when he heard a loud voice say: . . .

Cue: Voice of God
[Speak loudly and slowly; cup your hands around your mouth.]

Moses, you need to wash your feet! . . .
And while you are at it, I'd like you to tell Pharaoh
    to let my people go free.
And if you have any trouble, just use the staff I'll send you.
Shalom,
Yahweh.

Moses jumped up really excited . . . —higher— . . . because he had never been given a whole staff before. As he waited impatiently for his first applicant to show up, . . . his brother Aaron ran into him, . . . knocking both of them down. . . . Aaron helped Moses up and said in a voice similar to Bugs Bunny's: . . .

Cue: Aaron
[Speak like Bugs Bunny.]

Ummm, what's up, Moses?
Lookie here what I just found, a really neato staff!
And there's a small stone tablet attached that says,
    "Just stop, drop, and watch.
    Warranty expires after twelve uses.
    Shalom,
    Yahweh"
Hey, let's see what it can do. . . .

Aaron tossed the staff onto the ground, and it turned into a giant python that began to wrap itself around Moses, squeezing really tight, . . . causing his tongue to stick out and his eyes to grow big and wide. . . . Moses managed to gasp out these words in a squeaky voice: . . .

Cue: Moses
[Gasping for air]

Pretty . . . nice . . . staff, . . . Aaron. . . . Now . . . if . . . you . . . could . . . call . . . it . . . off . . . me, . . . I . . . think . . . we . . . need . . . to . . . go . . . see . . . a . . . pharaoh . . . about . . . some . . . frogs. . . .

The python turned back into the staff. Moses and Aaron picked it up and skipped over to the great Pharaoh, . . . who was drinking a glass of Nile water while squeezing the last bit of blood from a turnip. . . . Moses pointed the staff at Pharaoh and sang a message to him that went to the tune of "Louie, Louie": . . .

Cue: Moses
[Sing this to the tune of "Louie, Louie."]

Pharaoh, Pharaoh
Ohhh baby, let my people go.
Ugh!

Suddenly, Pharaoh's glass of water turned into blood, which got Pharaoh all choked up. . . . Remembering that he had both a hard heart and a hard head, Pharaoh stared back at Moses and Aaron, . . . cross-eyed, . . . and with defiance he said in his best Elmer Fudd voice: . . .

Cue: Pharoah
[Speak like Elmer Fudd.]

Why you wascally Hebwew you,
You'll never twick me into wetting your people go
I need them to finish building an eweventh bedwoom
    at my Summa home in Caiwo.

Moses looked baffled . . . because he couldn't understand a word Pharaoh had said. But Moses knew he was going to have to play hardball with him. Pharaoh, thinking the same thing, stepped into a pitcher's stance . . . then wound up . . . counterclockwise . . . three times . . . and, in slow motion, . . . threw a changeup to Moses, who slowly swung the staff. . . . As soon as Moses finished his swing, . . . the audience turned into frogs, . . . hopping up and down and making weird croaking sounds . . . and searching for bugs with their tongues. . . .

After the crowd settled down, . . . Pharaoh pitched two fastballs . . . at the same time, . . . with both hands. . . . But Moses was ready and hit both with his staff, . . . which made the right side of the audience fly around like gnats . . . and the left side like flies, . . . with both sides making irritating buzzing sounds in each other's ears. . . .

Pharaoh's next pitch was a curveball, . . . causing Moses to spin around with the staff before hitting it to the right side of the audience, . . . making the females on that side turn into mooing cows . . . and the males into neighing horses. . . . But the ball continued to curve to the left side of the audience, turning them into a repulsive and grotesque disease, . . . which swarmed around the cows and horses, . . . breathing in their faces . . . and causing them to slump over and die, frozen in really weird postures . . . —weirder than that even. . . .

The ball continued to curve around the room, hitting Pharaoh on the side of the head, . . . —the other side— . . . causing him to itch uncontrollably, . . . with ugly festering boils all over his neck, . . . his armpits, . . . his kneecaps, . . . and his rear end, . . . which caused the audience to become grossed out . . . and made Moses sing out his tune again: . . .

Cue: Moses
[Sing this to the tune of "Louie, Louie."]

Pharaoh, Pharaoh
Ohhh baby, let my people go.
Ugh!

Pharaoh was getting really agitated . . . and began jumping up and down, screaming bad things in Egyptian. . . . Moses tossed the staff to Aaron, . . . who pointed it at the left side of the audience, causing them to stomp their feet so loud it sounded like thunder. . . . Then he pointed it at the right side, . . . causing them to slap their laps so fast it sounded like hail falling down. . . . The noise got louder . . . and louder, . . . until Aaron called for a rain delay by waving the staff back and forth, . . . bringing about complete silence . . . for three days. . . .

Just when Pharaoh thought the game was over, Moses tossed a ball to Aaron, who smacked it with the staff, turning everyone into wild and crazy locusts, . . . hopping and buzzing all around the room . . . and messing up people's hair. . . . Then Moses and Aaron led everyone in singing to Pharaoh one more time: . . .

Cue: Moses and Aaron
[Sing this to the tune of "Louie, Louie."]

Pharaoh, Pharaoh
Ohhh baby, let my people go.
Ugh!

But Pharaoh's heart and head were still hard as a rock, . . . and he just shook his head and made mean faces at Moses and Aaron, . . . who shook their fingers back at Pharaoh, warning that the next hit would be his last.

At that moment, Moses pointed with his staff to the highest point of a nearby pyramid . . . as if he were going to hit the ball over it. This made Pharaoh laugh out loud . . . —even louder than that— . . . because no one, I mean NO ONE, had ever hit a ball over the pyramid before, which is why they called it the Green Monster.

So Moses made a big wager with Pharaoh that if he was able to knock the ball over the Green Monster, Pharaoh would have to give up all of his firstborn draft picks (except for the Lambs, the local Israelite team).

Pharaoh agreed with a sly smirk, . . . knowing that he was going to throw his illegal spitball. He then spat into his hand . . . and used it to brush back his hair, . . . which in turn greased up his entire palm, which he smeared all over the ball. . . . The audience gasped, . . . then held its breath . . . —longer . . . longer . . . longer— . . . until Pharaoh wound up and tossed the ball at Moses with all his might. . . . The eyes of the audience followed the pitch as it slowly slid its way toward Moses, . . . first this way, . . . then that way, . . . as Moses reached back with his staff . . . —further . . . further— . . . and swung with all his might. . . . The entire audience stood up as they watched the ball sail up . . . up . . . up . . . and over the Green Monster!

The crowd went wild, . . . while Moses and Aaron did a victory dance. . . . Then they lead the audience in singing three times their theme song: . . .

Cue: Moses and Aaron
[Sing this to the tune of "Louie, Louie."]

Pharaoh, Pharaoh
Ohhh baby, let my people go.
Ugh!
[Sing it two more times.]

To be continued . . .

Props

☐ a Bible with the readings marked
☐ signs displaying the boldfaced subheads for the commentaries

Reading and Commentaries

1. The story of Moses and the Exodus is told throughout the Book of Exodus. Summarize the key points and the ten plagues from the actual story, using the various passages below to give the audience a scriptural summary of the larger story.
• Yahweh's call to Moses to free the Israelites (Exodus 3:1–10)
• The giving of the staff to Moses (Exodus 4:1–5)
• Moses and Aaron being sent to Pharaoh (Exodus 7:1–6)
• Passover (the tenth and final plague) (Exodus 12:21–28)

2. After the reading summary, present the following commentaries to the group. Before you discuss each point, hand the sign displaying its subhead to the skit character it best applies to, and have that person stand in front of the group as you walk everyone through the meaning of the story.

God Chooses Moses

Moses is one of the major leaders and heroes of the Old Testament, and he continues to be so for both Christian and Jewish people today. However, he did not start out as a likely hero or prophet. He was described as someone who had difficulty speaking and spent years in hiding for killing an Egyptian who was mistreating an Israelite slave. During his hiding, he re-establishes his life as a family man and shepherd in Midian. It is here that he encounters Yahweh personally in a burning bush and hears God's name revealed for the first time: "I Am Who Am" (Exodus 3:14). From this moment on in history, God is seen as one who has a personal relationship with humanity. Yahweh tells Moses that he has been chosen as the one to set the Israelites free from their enslavement by Pharaoh.

God Provides Moses with Support

Moses's acceptance of God's call is not immediate. He has a number of reasons why he's not the one for the job. But God provides him with what he needs. First God gives him a staff to reveal the signs and to provide him with the authority and power that will allow him to speak with Pharaoh. Second God provides Moses with his brother Aaron as a supportive presence in helping him to get over his concerns about speaking publicly to both Pharaoh and the Israelites.

God Versus Gods

One of the biggest story lines occurring throughout the Book of Exodus is the battle between the many Egyptian gods and Yahweh, the God of the Israelites. During this time period, people believed that each country or area was ruled by the gods of that area, so that when one entered a new territory, they had to begin worshiping the particular gods recognized in that area. Moses tried to convince both Pharaoh and the Hebrew slaves that there is but one God, Yahweh, who is God of all ("I Am Who I Am") and who is not confined to any border, river, or boundary. This ongoing "battle" is played out in the unfolding of the ten plagues that are sent upon Pharaoh and the Egyptian people.

The Plagues

One can choose to examine the plagues through a variety of lenses: as miraculous events that happened as written, as the result of some natural phenomenon such as a comet striking Earth or a volcano erupting or the Nile flooding, or as a storytelling mode that helped to explain the struggle between Pharaoh's gods and Yahweh, the God of the Israelite patriarchs (Abraham, Isaac, and Jacob) and the God who revealed himself to Moses. No one knows for sure exactly how the plagues came about or whether they all did, which is doubtful because numerous inconsistencies exist among them. For example, the fifth plague was supposed to kill all the livestock belonging to the Egyptians, but the boils (sixth plague), hail (seventh plague), and death of firstborn (tenth plague) were also supposed to affect all the livestock, which would not have happened if they were all dead by the fifth plague.

Clearly the focus here is not on the historical truth, but on the deeper and more powerful biblical truths that arise from these series of stories. Namely that God intends to keep the promise to deliver God's people to a better place than they are now. The end result is the acknowledgment that there is only one God at work here: Yahweh, a God who knows no limits, no boundaries, and cannot be contained or controlled by humans. And because of that, in the final inning, God wins (and the crowd goes wild!).

(The commentary notes are based on Dianne Bergant, editor, *The Collegeville Bible Commentary: Old Testament,* pages 83–92.)

Props

☐ paper
☐ markers or pens, one for each small group

Reflection and Discussion

1. Divide into small groups of four to six people, and give each group a sheet of paper and a marker. Instruct them to develop a top ten list made up of ten ways (that is, "plagues") God might get a person's attention today if his or her heart was hardened like Pharaoh's. Encourage the groups to be both humorous and creative in their approach.

2. Invite each small group to share its list with the large group. Spend some time discussing what images of God these lists conjure up and if they accurately represent our current understanding of the nature of God.

1. Lead the group in a discussion of questions such as the ones that follow:
• God spoke to Moses through a burning bush. In what ways do you hear, feel, see, or experience God speaking to you or others in the world today? What is God's message?

- What "plagues" (consequences) might people today suffer from when they turn their back on God and God's presence in the world?
- Who today serves as a modern-day Moses, bringing God's message to those who are oppressing and enslaving others?
- God used Moses, an imperfect and flawed person, to do an impossible task. Spend a few moments in silence thinking about what impossible tasks God might be calling you to accept?

After a few minutes of silence, invite anyone who wishes to share a thought or reaction with the group to do so.

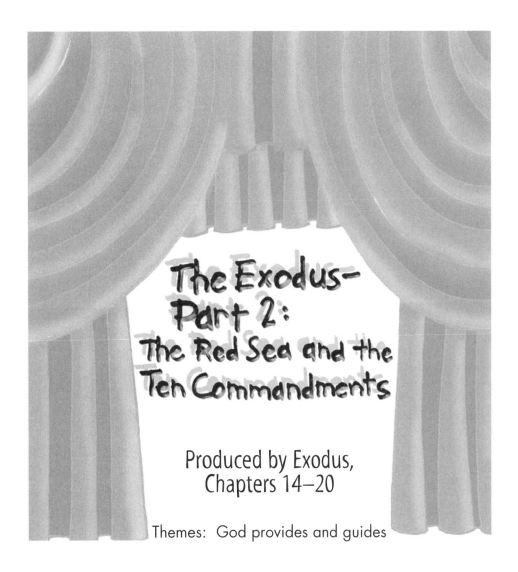

**The Exodus—
Part 2:
The Red Sea and the
Ten Commandments**

Produced by Exodus,
Chapters 14–20

Themes: God provides and guides

Synopsis

This Scripture skit continues the story of Moses and the Israelites as told in the Book of Exodus, covering their escape from
Pharaoh by crossing the Red Sea, their grumbling in the desert,
and the giving of the Law to the people through the Ten Commandments. As the audience members are led through this
journey, they are invited to recall an experience of liberation
and growth that has marked their own faith journey and to
examine God's presence through it all.

Props

☐ a small cup of water (Keep it near the audience and let
"Miriam" know where it is.)
☐ a staff (This could be any stick, broom, or mop that is
handy.)

Cast (7–10 people)

☐ Moses
☐ Aaron
☐ Miriam (Tell her where the cup of water has been placed.)
☐ three to six charioteers
☐ a complaining Hebrew (with a disgusting voice)
☐ the audience—the two sides of the Red Sea

If this is the first skit the group has done . . .
Explain that the characters selected are to do *exactly* what they hear the director read and are to be sure to face the audience during the performance. You should pause at each ellipsis (. . .) to give the characters time to do what you just read. When you come across a cue card, hold the book in front of the character who must read it, and point to the box containing the lines while emphasizing the voice in which it is to be read. Take your time and let the laughs roll!

During the skit, the audience will be instructed to do various things, which they should do when they hear it announced in the script.

Skit

Moses and Aaron were practicing singing "I'm a Little Teapot," . . . with hand motions, . . . when they heard a commotion from the audience. . . . Pharaoh had just agreed to let the Israelites go free! The audience went wild and jumped up from their seats, . . . then hopped on their right foot, . . . then their left foot, . . . then sat back down, . . . and did the wave . . . —one more time. . . .

Moses began packing up all his belongings . . . and placing them on Aaron's back. . . . First were the suitcases, . . . three of them, . . . then the table . . . and chairs, . . . and finally the kitchen sink. . . . The weight caused Aaron to squat as he walked alongside Moses, leading thousands of Israelites out of Egypt and toward the Red Sea, which is being played today by the audience. . . .

When they came to the Red Sea, . . . it was very choppy, . . . with waves rolling slowly from left to right . . . and back again. . . . Moses and Aaron, wanting to make a good impression, waved back. . . . Aaron happened to glance over his shoulder . . . —the other one— . . . just in time to see hundreds of charioteers off in the distance, . . . sharpening their swords . . . and plucking their nose hairs. . . . Moses and Aaron looked at each other in panic, . . . followed by hysteria, . . . causing them to pull on each other's hair. . . .

Their sister, Miriam, jumped into action, . . . picking up some water from the sea and splashing it on Moses and Aaron, . . . bringing them to their senses. . . . Miriam handed the staff to Moses, . . . but missed and hit Aaron. . . . Finally she put the stick in Moses's hand and pushed him toward the sea. . . .

Moses held the staff and opened his arms wide, . . . causing the entire sea to draw back in disgust as it held its nose with one hand . . . and its neighbor's with the other. . . . Then the sea slowly began to divide in the middle . . . —a little further even— . . . so that all the Israelites could pass through unharmed. . . .

The charioteers began galloping madly to the sea, . . . making a thunderous noise. . . . The noise caused the sea to swarm around the charioteers . . . and hug and tickle them until they cried "Yahweh." . . .

After the sea calmed down, . . . Moses, Aaron, and Miriam gave each other a high five . . . and led the people into the wilderness. . . . For days they walked in circles, . . . getting so dizzy they fell down asleep. . . .

In the morning, a complaining Hebrew took two giant steps forward, . . . followed by three baby hops, . . . and two tiptoes, . . . ending up right in front of Moses. The Hebrew, speaking in the most disgusting, irritating voice ever heard by humanity, said: . . .

Cue: Complaining Hebrews
[Speak in an irritating voice.]

Moses, ohhhh Moses . . .
What do you think we are supposed to eat and drink in this "promised land" of a desert you've dragged us into? We'd be better off as slaves in Egypt; at least we would have time for afternoon tea. All we do now is walk in circles and sleep. I wish you'd stop and ask directions—at this rate we'll be here forty years!

Moses looked up to God and pleaded for a hand. . . . Immediately Aaron and Miriam's hands covered the mouth of the complaining Hebrew, . . . and all in the room gave thanks. . . . Then God sent down some Wonder bread and Hi-C, and the crowd applauded, . . . jumping up and giving God a big cheer. . . .

In gratitude God sent down two stone tablets, which crashed into Moses and Aaron, . . . knocking them both out for the ten-count!

The end.

Props

☐ a Bible with the readings marked
☐ signs displaying the boldfaced subheads for the commentaries

Reading and Commentaries

1. The second part of the story of Moses (the crossing of the Red Sea, the journey into the wilderness, and the giving of the Ten Commandments) is told in chapters 14–20 of the Book of Exodus. You may want to use the following passages to give the audience a scriptural summary of the larger story:

- Crossing of the Red Sea (Exodus 14:10–30)
- Manna in the desert (Exodus 16:2–8
- Water from the rock (Exodus 17:2–7)
- The Ten Commandments (Exodus 20:1–17)

2. After the reading summary, present the following commentaries to the group. Before you discuss each point, hand the sign displaying its subhead to the skit character it best applies to, and have that person stand in front of the group as you walk everyone through the meaning of the story.

Tens of Thousands of Israelites . . . and One God

When we think about Pharaoh letting the Israelite slaves go free, we must imagine an entire town of people packing up as many belongings as they could carry and traveling for hundreds of miles in "tribes," small communities of people each headed up by elders. To move, govern, and feed such a large group requires an incredible amount of time and resources and does not occur without major difficulties and setbacks. But Exodus reminds us that through it all, God is present to the Israelites— appearing as a cloud by day and a pillar of fire by night, reminding them of Yahweh's constant presence and protection.

The Crossing of the Sea

Although the popular name for the sea that was crossed is the Red Sea, it is widely believed that it was actually referred to as the Sea of Reeds, so named for the many papyrus reeds that grew in the shallow, marshy area where the crossing likely took place. Exodus, chapter 14, actually contains two "tellings" of this peak experience in Israel's history. The more popular version highlights the dramatic image of Moses using his staff to divide the sea into two halves, allowing the Israelites to pass, but swallowing up the Egyptians. Another version is that Yahweh provides a strong easterly wind that pushes the shallow waters back through the night, allowing the Israelites to cross, but which clogs the heavier Egyptian chariots in the muddy ground, resulting in their eventual retreat. No matter which version of the story is told, the end result and theme is the same: *God liberated the Israelites from the slavery of Pharaoh.*

Caring for a Nation in the Wilderness

During the forty years that the Israelites spend wandering in the desert, story after story appears chronicling their fears, their complaints, and their trials and tribulations as they struggle to trust completely in God's graciousness. Each time they face a food or water shortage, God provides them with just enough to satisfy their needs. Through manna in the desert and water from rocks, the message to the people of faith is clear: God will provide! The Israelites, however, do not always grasp or trust in this message.

The Sinai Covenant and the Ten Commandments

It is at Mount Sinai that the Israelites form a lasting Covenant with Yahweh that is symbolized and summarized through the Ten Commandments. Mountains have always represented closeness to God in Jewish history, so it is no surprise that Moses goes up the mountain to speak with God. In so doing, Moses receives the Covenant from Yahweh, which calls the Israelites to be faithful to Yahweh just as Yahweh has been faithful to the Israelites, providing for their needs and protecting them from harm.

The first three commandments speak of loving and honoring God, whereas the last seven highlight how we are to treat our "neighbor." These last seven commandments likely evolved from tribal wisdom gleaned over many years of living in the wilderness. These laws helped the various tribes live together more peacefully and faithfully as a people. From then on, the Jewish people celebrated each year the giving of the Law to Moses and the Israelites as the feast of Pentecost.

(These commentary notes are based on Dianne Bergant, editor, *The Collegeville Bible Commentary: Old Testament*, pages 94–95.)

Props

☐ paper
☐ pens, one for each person

Reflection and Discussion

1. Explain to the group that after the Israelites were freed from their slavery and crossed the Red Sea, Miriam led the

group in a song of praise to Yahweh that recalled the powerful event (Exodus 15:20–21). Through song, the story of the Exodus could be passed down from generation to generation.

2. Form small groups of four to six people, and assign each one an event from the following list (add others as needed). Ask each group to discuss what facts they know about that event and to develop a poem (or song) that describes the triumph from the standpoint of those who were freed or liberated.
• The fall of the Berlin Wall and communism in the Soviet Union
• Ghandi helping India to gain independence from Britain
• The end of apartheid in South Africa
• The victory over Nazi Germany in World War II
• Minorities celebrating the passage of the Civil Rights Act
• Women getting the right to vote

3. When the small groups are done, invite each to share its poem or song with the large group, indicating why they chose to highlight the emotions and facts they did as well as why they chose to leave out other facts or emotions.

Discuss together the elements that were common to all the poems or songs. Ask: How might people of faith view these historical events through the eyes of faith?

1. Lead the group in a discussion of questions such as the ones that follow:
• Have you ever witnessed a "miraculous" event? What was it like to be a part of it?
• What are some ways that young people today are "oppressed" or "enslaved"? What are the causes and the cures for these experiences?
• What experience of liberation or freedom have you witnessed or experienced?
• Review the Ten Commandments. Which would you say are the most important for young people today to follow? Which are the most difficult for young people today to follow?
• Spend a few moments in silence reflecting on the Ten Commandments and which ones you need to focus on more in order to build a stronger relationship with God and others.

2. Give the young people a few minutes of silence to reflect on this session. Then invite those who wish to share any thought or reaction they have about this session to do so.

Elijah and the Prophets of Baal

Produced by
1 Kings 18:17–39

Themes: God versus gods,
faithfulness

Synopsis

This Scripture story uses the wonderful account of Elijah at Mount Carmel facing off with hundreds of priests of the god Baal in order to prove who the real God is. In examining this story, the audience is invited to consider who the lesser gods are within our contemporary culture today and how these may be luring people away from our one, true God.

Cast (6–8 people plus the entire audience)

☐ Elijah
☐ five to seven priests of Baal
☐ the audience

If this this is the first skit the group has done . . .
Explain that the characters selected are to do *exactly* what they hear the director read and are to be sure to face the audience during the performance. You should pause at each ellipsis (. . .) to give the characters time to do what you just read. When you come across a cue card, hold the book in front of the character who must read it, and point to the box containing the lines while emphasizing the voice in which it is to be read. Take your time and let the laughs roll!

Before reading the skit, instruct the audience to "boo" and "hiss" every time the "priests of Baal" are introduced or referred to. Read the whole script as if you are an excited announcer at a boxing or wrestling match.

Skit

[Speak in a boxing match announcer's voice.]

Ladiiiiieeees and Gentlemen, welcome to Mount Carmel, site of this Sunday's supremacy battle, featuring a contest of skill and power to determine who's God will reign. In this corner we have 450 overly confident priests of the popular god-of-the-moment, Baaaaal *("Boo! Hiss!")*, . . . and they sure brought a lot of bull with them.

And in the other corner, representing Yahweh, and Yahweh alone, is the prophet Elijah . . . along with . . . uh . . . well, it's just Elijah! . . . That's probably because the evil Queen Jezebel *("Boo! Hiss!")* . . . and mean King Ahab *("Boo! Hiss!")* . . . have already killed most of Yahweh's prophets. . . .

We're here to determine who is responsible for the three years of drought that have plagued our lands. . . . Is it Baaaal? *("Boo! Hiss!")* . . . Or is it Yahweh? . . . Today, one way or another, the truth will come out, and the false god will be revealed and wiped out.

Soooooo, arrrrrrrrrre you readyyyyyyyyyyyy toooooo rrrrrrrrumble!?

To determine whose God is in charge of things, we've prepared a cook-off, a veritable "Battle of the BBQ," if you will. Who will be able to fire up the ol' altar and prepare the best barbecued bull?

Will it be the 450 priests of Baal (*"Boo! Hiss!"*) . . . or Elijah all by himself? . . . Since there are 450 angry priests (*"Boo! Hiss!"*) . . . and only one restroom up here on Mount Carmel, what say we let them go first?

It looks like the priests are trying to build a pyramid out of themselves, . . . but it keeps falling down . . . and again. . . . Now they appear to be arguing over who should be at the top. . . . Wait! . . . It almost sounds like they are complaining to Baal: . . .

Cue: Priests of Baal
[*Whine together over and over again in an annoying chant.*]

Ohhhhh Baaaaaal,
Wherefore art thou, oh mighty Baaaaaal?

Elijah is just standing there in total defiance, . . . tapping his foot . . . —the other one— . . . and staring at his sundial . . . over and over again. . . . Now he's beginning to mock them . . . by humming some sort of tune, . . . which sounds like "I Can't Get No Satisfaction." . . .

Folks, it's been over four hours now and the priests (*"Boo! Hiss!"*) are completely frustrated that Baal has not lit the fire for the barbecue yet. . . . They appear to be tiring from all their chanting and pyramid building . . . and, wait, I can't believe it, . . . they've just plopped down on the floor . . . and are throwing their hands up in the air . . . and . . . and . . . they are just leaving their hands up there! . . .

Now Elijah is walking around the priests in circles, . . . mocking and taunting them. . . . Let's listen in to see what he's saying: . . .

Cue: Elijah
[Speak each line separately and in a mocking, teasing voice.]

Soooooooo, anyone got a light?
How's that barbecue coming along?
Maybe Baal is so old that he's taking a nap?
Maybe you should chant a little LOUDER?
Maybe he's vacationing at Disney World and doesn't want to be BOTHERED?
Or is he at his knitting club today?

Looks like that last comment really got to the priests (*"Boo! Hiss!"*). . . . They are pulling out their hair, . . . and now they are lying down on the floor . . . and throwing temper tantrums. . . .

Okay, folks, it looks like it's Elijah's turn to see what he and his God, Yahweh, might be able to fire up. . . . He's motioning for the priests to sit in a circle on the floor, . . . facing inward, . . . and looking at one another. . . . Now Elijah appears to be circling around them, . . . on the outside, . . . patting each one on the head as he passes them by. . . . Wait a second . . . he's play-ing "duck, duck, goose" with them, . . . and boy does he have their goose. . . . He is showing them today that he isn't one to be trifled with. . . .

Now it appears as if he's pouring water around the circle of priests, . . . lots of water . . . —even more than that. . . . Why would he possibly want to use water when he needs to start a fire to cook the barbecue? The priests are just as puzzled as we are, . . . scratching their heads . . . and rubbing their stomachs at the same time. . . .

Wait! . . . It looks as if Elijah is ready to call out to Yahweh: . . .

Cue: Elijah
[Speak in a commanding voice.]

Lord, God of Abraham, Isaac, and Jacob,
Let your light shine forth this day.
And for all that we are about to eat, may we be truly thankful.
Amen!

WOW! Look at that flash of light. . . . It has just ignited that water like it was oil. . . . Do you believe in miracles? . . . The audience is going wild! . . . And now the priests are doing that "we're not worthy" worshiping thing to Elijah. . . .

Ladies and gentlemen, this is a stunning upset! Who would have thought that one person with a lot of water could have lit that fire. Elijah is now doing his victory dance . . . and a well deserved one it is. Wait, he's now pointing upward, . . . suggesting that it wasn't his doing. . . . No, someone greater than he made this happen. . . .

And to top it off, it's now just started raining . . . hard. . . . Yes, the drought is over folks, Yahweh rules! And the crowd goes wild!

The end.

Props

☐ a Bible with the reading marked
☐ signs displaying the boldfaced subheads for the commentaries

Reading and Commentaries

1. Invite someone to proclaim 1 Kings 18:17–39.

2. After the reading, present the following commentaries to the group. Before you discuss each point, hand the sign displaying its subhead to the skit character it best applies to, and have that person stand in front of the group as you walk everyone through the meaning of the story.

Elijah

Elijah is considered the father of the prophets, being one of the first and greatest of the prophets of Israel to boldly call the kingdom and its leaders back to its Covenant with Yahweh. Elijah, whose name means "Yahweh is my God," spends his life proving just that, especially in the face of some tough and outrageous opposition, as this story illustrates.

Over the years, Elijah's name became synonymous with the hard words of the prophets, just as Moses's name recalled all that the Law encompassed. In fact, Elijah and Moses were often referred to in the same breath to call to mind all that God asked of Jews during Jesus's time. This is one of the reasons their presence alongside Jesus during the Transfiguration was such a powerful and symbolic event.

The Situation

Elijah lived during Old Testament times (before Jesus), when the Jews were divided into two separate kingdoms, one in the north and another in the south. Both strayed from Yahweh and began worshiping other gods, such as Asherah and Baal. When this story takes place, King Ahab and Queen Jezebel are the current, and very evil, rulers of the northern kingdom, the worst of the worst, mainly because they have chosen to turn away from Yahweh and worship another god, Baal. They even erect a temple to him in the capital. Then they begin to kill all of the prophets, or followers of Yahweh, who protest against them.

Why the Drought?

As the story unfolds, a three year drought has struck the land and Elijah and King Ahab finally meet on Mount Carmel to decide whose sins are responsible for the drought: Elijah's or Ahab's? But the actual contest is to decide who the real God is: Yahweh or Baal?

Unfair Numbers

Elijah arrives for the showdown by himself, but he asks that King Ahab send all of the priests of Baal, numbering some 450, along with 400 priests of another god, Asherah, to compete against his God, Yahweh. By stacking the numbers so unfairly (850 to 1), Yahweh's victory in the end leaves no doubt who the real God is.

A Symbolic Contest

The contest between Elijah and the priest was symbolic of an individual, as well as a collective, struggle that Israel was experiencing between who to worship: one or more of the many gods throughout the land, or the one God, Yahweh, who had led them out of slavery and to the Promised Land years before. It might seem an easy choice today, yet even now, many fall victim to the lure and lust of other gods who seem to offer a life or lifestyle that is more rewarding and less demanding than that of the Lord God. But in the end, it's the same as on Mount Carmel—the other gods are all smoke and no fire!

(The commentary notes are based on Dianne Bergant, editor, *The Collegeville Bible Commentary: Old Testament*, pages 308–309.)

Props

☐ newsprint and markers
☐ a sheet of newsprint containing the following phrases:
  • I am _____, the god of _____
  • Worship me and I will make you . . .
  • I will be your god if you will . . .
  • You can find me at . . .
  • What makes me grow stronger and bigger is . . .
  • That which diminishes or destroys me is . . .

Reflection and Discussion

1. Arrange the participants into small groups of three to four and distribute two sheets of newsprint and a few markers to each group.

2. Instruct the small groups to spend the next 15 to 20 minutes developing a "god" that people of our culture today tend to worship, and then to complete the sentences outlined on the newsprint based on that particular "god." An example is provided here:
• I am Mediavore, the god of all that can be.
• Worship me and I will help make everything look better than it is.
• I will be your god if you will watch me and only me.

- You can find me everywhere: in every home on computers, televisions, and radios, and on every billboard and magazine rack you pass.
- What makes me grow stronger and bigger is your undivided attention and unquestioning belief.
- That which diminishes or destroys me is when you turn away or start to question my motives and ask critical questions about who controls me.

3. When the small groups have completed step 2, ask them to develop on a second sheet of newsprint an image or likeness of the idol that might be erected by those who worship this god. Then have them transfer the written responses from step 2 onto strategic locations on the newsprint image.

In the example provided above for the god Mediavore, the group might draw a huge TV set with hypnotizing eyes. On the top of the television the group might place the god's name, and inside the screen the group might fill in the promise and lure and strength responses, while placing the weakness response underneath or to the side of the television.

4. When all the groups are done, invite a representative from each group to share its god-of-the-moment image and then to post it on the wall.

5. After all the small groups have shared, ask one of the young people to use a blank sheet of newsprint to record the answers by the large group to each question again, but this time referring to the Lord, our God (rather than idol gods). When you come to a statement that does not apply to Yahweh, such as, "I will be your god if you will . . ." try to get the group to say that it doesn't apply and then invite them to say what type of promise does apply (that is, an unconditional promise to be our God and we, his people).

CURTAIN call

1. Lead the group in a discussion of the following questions:
- What do all the god-of-the-moments have in common?
- What is so attractive or alluring about them?
- What is different from the description of the other gods and that of our one God?
- What is unpopular in today's culture about worshiping a relentless God who challenges and loves us unconditionally?

- Which god-of-the-moment are young people most drawn to? Which one are you personally most drawn to?
- Who are the prophetic voices in today's world that call us back to worshiping the one, true God? Which of these speaks most clearly to you? Why?

2. After a few minutes of silence, invite the participants to pray by responding as they wish to the following sentence: Lord, help us to forsake the gods of . . .

3. Conclude by offering the following prayer:

As we turn our back to these lesser gods,
give us the strength to proclaim your presence
by the way we live our lives and walk our faith.
We ask this through the God of Abraham, Isaac, and Jacob,
the Father of our Lord Jesus Christ, to whom we now pray,
Our Father, who art in heaven . . . [continue with the Lord's Prayer].

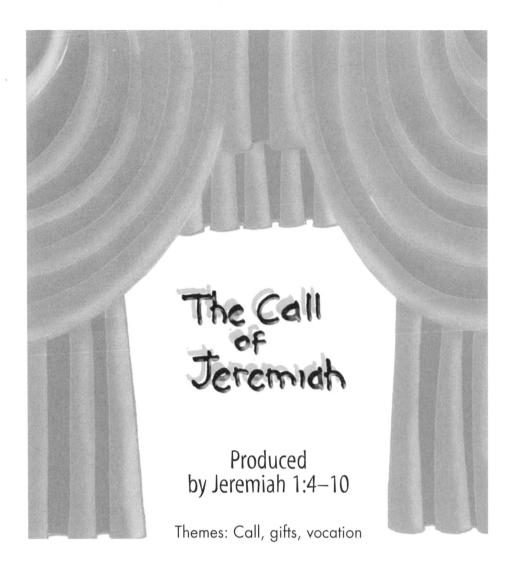

The Call of Jeremiah

Produced
by Jeremiah 1:4–10

Themes: Call, gifts, vocation

Synopsis

This Scripture story invites the participants to consider the gifts God has instilled in them and how God may be calling each of them to use these gifts faithfully in the years ahead.

Cast (6–10 people)

☐ Jeremiah
☐ the Word of God (who speaks like a cowgirl)
☐ a group of two or four girls
☐ a group of two or four guys

DIRECTOR'S NOTES

It is likely (and intentional) that the audience will not understand what Jeremiah is saying at first. If so, repeat the cue card line as instructed in the parentheses following each of his lines.

If this is the first skit the group has done . . .
Explain that the characters selected are to do *exactly* what they hear the director read and are to be sure to face the audience during the performance. You should pause at each ellipsis (. . .) to give the characters time to do what you just read. When you come across a cue card, hold the book in front of the character who must read it, and point to the box containing the lines while emphasizing the voice in which it is to be read. Take your time and let the laughs roll!

Skit

Jeremiah was a typical teenager, with curious eyes, . . . a stomach that always growled, . . . and big feet that caused him to trip a lot. . . . Besides these great qualities, Jeremiah had one other noticeable characteristic that set him apart from the rest of the crowd: he could speak only while sticking out his tongue. . . . For example, he would approach a group of girls hoping to tell them how nice they looked, and it would end up sounding like this: . . .

Cue: Jeremiah
[Speak while sticking out our tongue.]

Hey, ladies, you are looking particularly fetching today. Want to go for a walk?

(Translated this means, "Hey, ladies, you are looking particularly fetching today. Want to go for a walk?"). Jeremiah's speech always made the ladies giggle so hard that they would shake, . . . uncontrollably, . . . causing them to sound like a gaggle of geese. . . .

At other times, Jeremiah would make his way over to the temple corner, where the guys would hang out practicing their latest dance moves. . . . On this day they were teaching each other how to do the waltz. . . . (Waltz music, please).

Jeremiah tripped over to them, . . . wanting to learn to dance as well as they did, so he asked: . . .

Cue: Jeremiah
[Speak while sticking out your tongue.]

Hey, guys, that dance appears pretty peculiar.
Perhaps you could teach me a step or two.

(Translated this means: "Hey, guys, that dance appears pretty peculiar. Perhaps you could teach me a step or two.") . . . But Jeremiah's request so confused the guys that when they began to dance again, . . . they kept bumping into each other . . . and stepping on each other's toes. . . . This made them glare at Jeremiah with anger, . . . followed by exasperation, ... ending up with the whole group making a loud sigh of disgust. . . . Then off they pirouetted to join the girls, who were still giggling uncontrollably. . . .

Jeremiah slumped off, shaking his head and saying over and over again: . . .

Cue: Jeremiah
[Speak while sticking out your tongue.]

Why was I put on this earth in the first place?
Why was I put on this earth in the first place?
Why was I put on this earth in the first place?

(Translated, this means, "Why was I put on this earth in the first place?")

Just then the Word of God came skipping around the room, . . . letting out a loud western "Yee haw!" . . . and ending up nose to nose with Jeremiah, . . . causing Jeremiah to lean way back, . . . —even further— . . . so he could say: . . .

Cue: Jeremiah
[Speak while sticking out your tongue.]

Who are you and what do you want of me?

The Word of God, sounding like a Western cowgirl, said: . . .

Cue: The Word of God
[Speak like a western cowgirl.]

Listen up, pardner . . .
Before the Lord God formed ya in your momma's womb,
God knew ya—inside and out,
Even those big feet and that peeeeculiar speech of yours.
And there's somethin' else God knows,
So listen up real careful-like. . . .

This caused Jeremiah to lean forward . . . —even more— . . .
placing his ear really close to the Word of God, who said: . . .

Cue: The Word of God
[Speak like a western cowgirl.]

[Really loud] God wants ya to be a prophet to the nations!

Jeremiah fell down and covered his ears, not knowing how to re-spond because the city had banned him from speaking in public and, perhaps even worse, he was a freshman.

The Word of God knew Jeremiah's thoughts and fears, so she pulled him up . . . and told him to hold on to his tongue. Then she said: . . .

Cue: The Word of God
[Speak like a Western cowgirl.]

Stop complainin' that yer only a boy.
When God calls you to do somethin',
Why then, ya better listen up and *just do it*!
And God's callin' ya to go out there and speak like a prophet.
And while yer at it; keep in mind one more thing, . . .
DON'T BE AFRAID!
'Cause God's now here—has been and always will be.
Do ya hear what I'm sayin?
Are ya catchin' my drift?
Well, then speak up . . .

And that's when Jeremiah began to feel that God *was* with him. . . . In fact, Jeremiah seemed taller, . . . braver, . . . and really quite handsome. . . . So he took two big steps to the center of the room, . . . followed by two baby steps . . . and one hop, . . . and spun around so he ended up facing the girls and guys who had mocked him before. Then he spoke: . . .

Cue: Jeremiah
[Speak in a deep, commanding voice.]

Here I am, Lord, ready to do your will!

This caused the guys to fall into the girls' arms, . . . and the girls to drop the guys, . . . so that they could let out a big "Yee haw!" for Jeremiah. . . .

The end.

Props

☐ a Bible with the reading marked
☐ signs displaying the boldfaced subheads for the commentaries

Reading and Commentaries

1. Invite someone to proclaim Jeremiah 1:4–10.

2. After the reading, present the following commentaries to the group. Before you discuss each point, hand the sign displaying its subhead to the skit character it best applies to, and have that person stand in front of the group as you walk everyone through the meaning of the story.

The Prophet's Role

A prophet was first and foremost a messenger of God. The prophet's role was to speak God's truth, sometimes forcefully and other times gently, depending on the situation, but always with the goal of calling people back into a right relationship with God. That is why this first section of Jeremiah is so important, because it describes Jeremiah's call, or commissioning, by God to speak God's word.

Prophets are generally not liked or respected until long after they are dead because their words are challenging and their persistence is strong. Jeremiah, Isaiah, and Ezekiel are considered the major prophets of the Old Testament because their books are the longest, but the Old Testament contains fifteen other prophetic books (referred to as minor because of their shorter length). Each prophet has his own style, but the message is always the same: *repent and return with all your heart, soul, and mind to the covenant you have with God.*

A Surprising Call

Jeremiah was hardly the most likely candidate to be a prophet. He was a young teenager, he stumbled along in his speech, and he lacked confidence in his gifts and abilities. When he heard God calling to him, he had plenty of excuses (and some pretty valid ones!) as to why he should not or could not respond to the call. But God assured him that he would not be left alone and that God's words would flow from his mouth.

A Tough Assignment

Things began easily enough for Jeremiah because the current leader of Israel, King Josiah, was a good king and pushed for religious reform. But when he unexpectedly died in a battle, his successors (Kings Jehoiakim and Zedekiah) were anything but good. Their hunger for power made them corrupt and ruthless in their leadership, which required Jeremiah to speak all the more fervently for repentance. Neither of these leaders cared for the truth that Jeremiah spoke, and more than once Jeremiah was beaten and arrested. Once he was tortured and left to die at the bottom of a well. But Jeremiah and his message survived, and he continued to call the people to return to a life pleasing to God.

Jeremiah and Jesus

Few people from the Old Testament have more in common with Jesus than Jeremiah. Both were rejected by their own people; both used parables to teach and call for reform; both predicted the fall of the Jerusalem Temple (Jeremiah by the Babylonians in 587 and Jesus by the Romans in AD 70); both had challenging messages for those in power; and both were beaten, tortured, and sentenced to death. These similarities caused many in Jesus's day to wonder if he were Jeremiah coming back from the dead (see Matthew 16:14).

(The commentary notes are based on Dianne Bergant, editor, *The Collegeville Bible Commentary: Old Testament,* page 454.)

Props

☐ newsprint and markers, one of each for each participant
☐ masking tape
☐ a tape or CD player and a tape or CD of reflective music

Reflection and Discussion

1. Explain to the group that Jeremiah was called at a young age to do something that he felt completely unprepared for—to speak boldly and courageously to leaders about how they had gotten off track with God. But God knew Jeremiah before he was even born, planting the gift of a prophetic voice in him, which he discovered as a teenager.

Ask questions such as the following:

• What special gift might God have planted in you to be discovered in your teen years?
• How might you "uncover" this gift?
• What type of life and lifestyle is God calling you to?

2. Distribute a sheet of newsprint and a marker to each participant, and ask the participants to write their name at the top, followed by the following phrase:

• "(name), a gift from God . . . called to . . . "

Direct the participants to place a line down the middle of their paper between "a gift from God" and "called to."

3. Provide the participants each with a piece of masking tape, inviting them to hang their sheet on a wall where the other participants can reach it and write on it (they may all place their sheets on the floor or tables if wall space is not available).

4. Tell the participants to go to each sheet of newsprint in the room and consider who that person is. Direct them to think about the person and the gifts that he or she might have, as well as how these gifts might be used to serve God in the coming years. For example: Someone may be quiet and observant of others, trying to be helpful when he or she sees a need. This gift might be used to serve those in need as a woman or male religious, a missionary, a volunteer in a Catholic Worker house, or a social worker.

Remind the participants to fill in both columns on each person's sheet (both the gifts they see in the individual and some of the potential ways that person might be called to use those gifts in the future). Tell them to be sure to write something on every person's paper and to take their time and be respectful and insightful with their comments.

Note: If this is a large group of more than ten participants, or the group does not know one another well enough to do this task, divide the large group into smaller sections by grade level or school or other similar groupings so they can focus on those they may know best.

Play some popular or reflective music while the young people fill in each other's sheets. Ask them not to read their own until instructed.

5. Once everyone has written on each sheet, invite the participants to take down their poster and to spend a few minutes reading and reflecting on what others see in them. Then proceed to the "Curtain Call" questions for processing this activity.

1. Lead the group in a discussion of the following questions:

- As you read your poster, share one thing that affirmed you and one thing that surprised you and why.
- Why is it that others see gifts in us that we sometimes do not see?
- What does this tell us about the nature of God and how we might hear or discern God's call in our lives?

2. Direct the young people to quietly re-examine their poster for the "surprise" that God may be calling them to. Then invite the group to offer spontaneous prayers with the response being, "Lord, open our ears so that we may hear your voice."

Suggest that the participants take their poster home and consider hanging it on their bedroom wall or ceiling to remind them of the gifts they possess and how God may be inviting them to use their gifts in the years ahead.

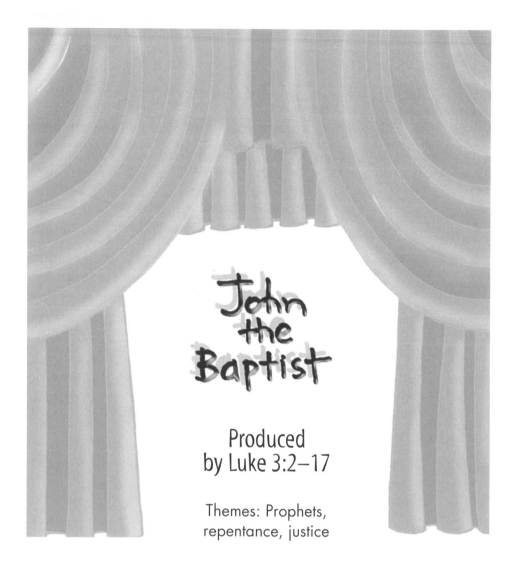

John
the
Baptist

Produced
by Luke 3:2–17

Themes: Prophets,
repentance, justice

Synopsis

This Scripture story examines the role of John the Baptist and his message of repentance, inviting the audience to consider that same message for their own lives as well as for the world today.

ACT ONE
ENGAGE

Props

☐ a cup of water (no more than one full cup)

Cast (8 people)

☐ John the Baptist (who speaks like a cowboy)
☐ two members of the crowd (who stay in their seats until called)
☐ two tax collectors (one who speaks like Goofy)
☐ two soldiers (who speak like Darth Vader)
☐ a horse

If this is the first skit the group has done . . .
Explain that the characters selected are to do *exactly* what they hear the director read and are to be sure to face the audience during the performance. You should pause at each ellipsis (. . .) to give the characters time to do what you just read. When you come across a cue card, hold the book in front of the character who must read it, and point to the box containing the lines while emphasizing the voice in which it is to be read. Take your time and let the laughs roll!

Give the cup of water to the character playing John, quietly telling him that he will be asked to use it throughout the skit to sprinkle water at people by dipping his fingers in the cup, but that he *must* save some for the very end of the skit.

Skit

One day John was out sprinkling his desert lawn with a cup of water, . . . when a sudden urge came upon him to sprinkle the audience. . . . Having their complete attention, he began to speak to them in a voice like a cowboy: . . .

> **Cue: John the Baptist**
> ***[Speak like a cowboy.]***
>
> Listen up, pilgrims,
> You need to prepare the way for the Lord.
> And that means raising up valleys and leveling mountains,
> Straightening out those pesky crooked lines
> And smoothin' over them there rough spots.
> Now this is no easy task, but it's sure being made a might harder
> 'Cause of a bunch of yellow-bellied, sap-suckin' hypocrites
>   like those Pharisees and Saducees over there.
> So if you want to make things right,
> I suggest ya get down off your high falutin' horses
> And get yourselves baptized in that Jordan River over yonder.

Two people from the crowd jumped forward . . . —a little further— . . . and asked John what they could do to help prepare the way. John told them to exchange shoes with one another . . . and do a tap dance . . . while singing "Row, Row, Row Your Boat" to the audience. . . . John then sprinkled them with some water . . . and told them to give all of their money to the people in the back row. . . . This delighted the back row so much that they stood up, . . . joined hands, . . . and did a red rover chant for the two people to join them. . . .

Next, two tax collectors tiptoed toward John, . . . cracking their knuckles . . . and flaring their nostrils. . . . They had greedy eyes . . . and large overbites . . . that made them talk like Goofy, as the shorter of the two said: . . .

> **Cue: Short Tax Collector**
> **[Speak like Goofy.]**
>
> Hey, John, uh . . .
> Golly gee. We are despised and goofy tax collectors!
> What can we do to straighten things out?

John looked at them with a distorted face, . . . filled with agonizing disgust, . . . and then coughed up a locust, . . . followed by a praying mantis, . . . and a large ball of camel hair. . . . Regaining his composure, he told them: . . .

> **Cue: John the Baptist**
> **[Speak like a cowboy.]**
>
> You tax collectors gotta stop overcharging these pilgrims.
> Sure ya gotta collect them taxes,
> And sure we all hate that,
> But don't you dare take more than is due,
> Or you'll find that this town ain't big enough for the three of us.

With that, John sprinkled the tax collectors with some water, . . . and off they skipped, . . . smiling and singing "Itsy Bitsy Spider" . . . with hand motions. . . .

Next, two soldiers fought their way toward John, . . . stepping on each other's toes . . . and slapping each other's hands like little girls. . . . Then the tallest of them spoke up in a voice like Darth Vader: . . .

Cue: Tall Soldier
[Speak like Darth Vadar.]

Tell us, John [*slow, heavy breath*].
We are soldiers [*slow, heavy breath*].
What should we do [*slow, heavy breath*]
if the Empire should strike back [*slow, heavy breathing*]?

John made the soldiers drop to the ground and count out ten push-ups . . . —in Spanish— . . . then told them: . .

Cue: John the Baptist
[Speak like a cowboy.]

Well, big fellas,
Quit your whinin' about what you are paid.
Be happy you got a job and do somethin' good with your money.
And don't give it to those folks in the back row,
'Cause they already got somethin' comin' to them
If you know what I mean!

With that, John ran to the back row . . . and sprinkled them with water. . . . This caused them to become filled with the Spirit, jumping up from their seats and shouting "Hallelujah!" . . . Then John returned to center stage and said to the crowd: . . .

Cue: John the Baptist
[Speak like a cowboy.]

Some of you think I'm the Grand Duke,
But I'm here to tell you that there's one coming soon
Who is so great and powerful,
I'm not even fit to polish his saddle,
Much less take off his boots.
Sure I sprinkled a little water and taught ya' a thing or two,
But he will baptize you in the Holy Spirit
And divide the sheep from the goats.
And trust me, pilgrims, you don't want to end up a goat!

With that, John whistled for his horse, . . . which neighed and stomped its hooves . . . as it galloped around the room, . . . stopping in front of John and bowing. . . . John bowed back and patted the horse on the head, saying: . . .

Cue: John the Baptist
[Speak like a cowboy.]

You know, ol' buddy,
Since I coughed up my locust and wild honey sandwich earlier,
A horse burger's sounding pretty tasty right now!

Hearing that, the horse reared up, knocking John to the floor, . . . causing him to baptize himself with the remainder of the water. . . . And the crowd shouted, "Hallelujah!" . . .

The end.

Props

☐ a Bible with the reading marked
☐ signs displaying the boldfaced subheads for the commentaries

Reading and Commentaries

1. Invite someone to proclaim Luke 3:2–17.

2. After the reading, present the following commentaries to the group. Before you discuss each point, hand the sign displaying its subhead to the skit character it best applies to, and have that person stand in front of the group as you walk everyone through the meaning of the story.

Waiting for the Messiah

It had been over three hundred years since the Jews had last heard a prophet's voice, and hope was high that a messiah would soon come. So when John arrived on the scene, the hearts of the people, and not just the Jews, burned with a renewed passion. Tax collectors, soldiers, and Gentiles alike came to hear him speak, so vast was the word spreading that John *might* just be the long-awaited Messiah because of the authenticity with which he both lived and spoke his message. He was a "wild man," a man from the wilderness who lived, ate, and dressed simply and whose passionate message for people to change their heart was hard to ignore.

John the Conscience Stinger

John called it as he saw it and spared no one's feelings. His mission was to wake people up, to sting their individual and collective consciences. His was a call to righteousness, challenging people to get "right" with God, to repent from the things that separated them from God. It did not matter to John who or what needed to be righted; religious leaders, Romans, Jews, and even King Herod himself were all recipients of John's no-holds-barred, stinging message of repentance. The Jewish word for repent *(teshubah)* literally means "to turn." So John's call to repent required that the people begin to *turn away* from evil and sin and *turn toward* the Light, who was soon coming.

A Window, Not a Wall

John was careful to let everyone know that he was *not* the Messiah, that one greater than he would soon be coming to change the world. This was a message he had to preach constantly because so many desperately wanted to believe that he was the long-awaited Anointed One. But John was adamant that he was merely a window to God. People had to be able to see through him to something beyond, something greater and more important than himself. This was where John's true greatness shone, in his ultimate humility to be totally obedient to the role God called him to play in Christ's coming. When he said he was not even fit to unstrap the sandals of the One who was to come, he was expressing complete servitude to God, because only the lowest slave—the non-Jewish slave—could be required to unstrap a sandal, and John placed himself beneath even this person!

Preparing the Way

There were very few well-maintained roads in Judea at this time in history. Most were worn paths or rutted trails. King Solomon, however, in building the Jerusalem Temple hundreds of years before, had commanded that all roads leading to the Temple be constructed from basalt stones and be made level so that all who entered Jerusalem would know that something special lay ahead. In fact, the only roads created and maintained back then were for use by the king, known as the "King's Highway." When the King planned to visit an area, messengers were sent ahead to spread the word that the people needed to prepare the way for the king. This is exactly what John was doing, spreading the word that people needed to prepare the way for the King of Kings.

The Threshing Floor

John used the image of the threshing floor and winnowing fork to help people understand what the Messiah would do when he came into the world. Once the wheat was harvested and the grain was separated into piles, a final task needed to happen to separate the unusable chaff from the good wheat. Farmers would use large winnowing forks, or shovels, to pick up large piles of grain and toss them into the air, where the light chaff would get blown away by the wind as the heavy grain fell to the threshing floor. The good grain was then collected and stored in barns, while the chaff was swept up and used as fuel for fires. John was saying that a similar separation would occur when the Messiah comes. Those who have repented, who have turned their lives toward God, would be saved, but those who have chosen to turn away from God would find their final destiny in an eternal fire.

(The commentary notes are based on Robert Karris, editor, *The Collegeville Bible Commentary: New Testament*, pages 943–944, and William Barclay, *Barclay's Daily Bible Study Series*.)

Props

☐ scrap paper
☐ markers or pens, one for each person

Reflection and Discussion

1. Arrange the participants into small groups of four to six people, and assign each group one or more roles or positions from the following list, so that all the roles on the list are assigned to a small group.
• military and police officials
• politicians and government officials
• church leaders
• employers
• laborers
• poor and vulnerable people
• parents
• teenagers

2. Ask each group to imagine that John the Baptist has come today to their town, and their assigned groups of people have come to him to ask what they should do or stop doing in order to be in a right relationship with God. Have the small groups discuss what John's response would be for each assigned role, and then be prepared to share this with the large group in 5 minutes.

3. Bring the small groups back together to share their responses. After each group shares, ask the others if they have anything to add or if anyone wishes to challenge what was said in terms of what John the Baptist might have actually preached.

Conclude by asking the group if these types of messages are being proclaimed today in their local area, and if not, why not?

CURTAIN call

1. Lead the group in a discussion of the following questions:

- Who would you classify as modern John the Baptists, prophets who live the truth they speak and call others to live it? What makes them "prophetic"?
- Why do people seem attracted to prophets—people who say it like it is and who seem to stir up our conscience? What are people searching for or seeking from them?
- What or who are the valleys that need to be raised in your community? What or who are the mountains that need to be made low? What needs to happen for everyone to be at the same level?
- Spend a few minutes quietly reflecting on what type of repentance John the Baptist is asking of you. In other words, what areas in your life do you need to turn away from in order to begin walking toward God?

After a couple of minutes, ask the group to share a prayer to God for what they need in their life to begin to turn toward God.

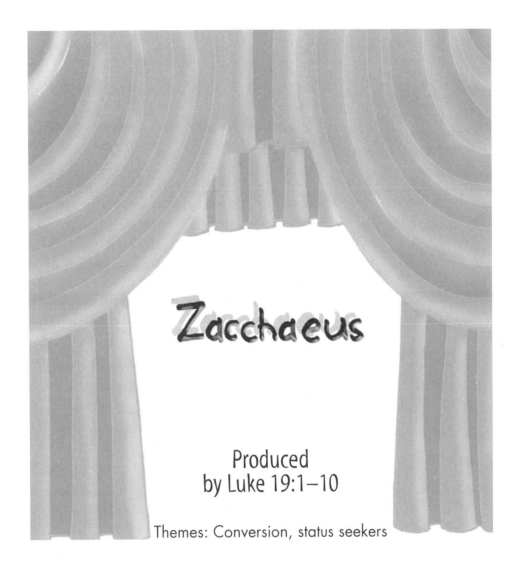

Zacchaeus

Produced
by Luke 19:1–10

Themes: Conversion, status seekers

Synopsis

This Scripture story invites the audience to examine the power structures and social orders they find themselves in and to reflect on how Jesus invites them to break free from those structures in order to experience his presence and forgiveness.

Cast (8 people plus the entire audience)

☐ Zacchaeus (a.k.a. Zack)
☐ a woman of the village
☐ a fisherman
☐ Jesus
☐ two disciples
☐ the tree (two people kneeling on one knee with hands joined)
☐ the people of Jericho (the remainder of the audience)

If this is the first skit the group has done . . .

Explain that the characters selected are to do *exactly* what they hear the director read and are to be sure to face the audience during the performance. You should pause at each ellipsis (. . .) to give the characters time to do what you just read. When you come across a cue card, hold the book in front of the character who must read it, and point to the box containing the lines while emphasizing the voice in which it is to be read. Take your time and let the laughs roll!

Instruct the audience that they are to do whatever the townsfolk or villagers are instructed to do during the skit. Tell them that every time they hear the phrase "tax collector" they are to boo and hiss (practice a couple of times before you begin the skit).

Skit

Zack was the shortest person in Jericho . . . —shorter than that even. . . . His face had a diabolic, twisted look to it, . . . which resembled the Grinch. . . . He had the voice of a munchkin . . . and the heart of a snail, . . . make that a flea, . . . actually more like a dust mite. . . .

Zack lived in Jericho, where he was the chief tax collector ("Boo! Hiss!"). . . . His real name was Zacchaeus, but because only the people in the front could pronounce it, . . . and only the last person to my right could spell it, . . . the people of Jericho just called him Zack, . . . that is, when they were speaking to him at all.

Usually when Zack walked by, the people of Jericho just made loud sounds with every step he took, . . . causing him much embarrassment. . . . Other times, the women of the town would turn their backs on him, . . . while the men would get down on their knees and sing, "Follow the Yellow Brick Road" in Munchkin voices. . . . Even though Zack was rich, he remained a hated and despised tax collector ("Boo! Hiss!"), . . . which made him feel very poor . . . and sad . . . and lonely . . . and empty . . . and shallow . . . and sick . . . and tired. . . . This led to a bad case of blisters all over the tip of his nose, . . . causing all the women to scream in horror. . . .

One day there was a commotion in the village . . . —even more commotion than that. . . . People were jumping up and down trying to see over one another. . . . A woman of the village began leaping around the room, screaming like she had just seen a famous Hollywood star. . . . She ended up right next to Zack as she screamed: . . .

Cue: Woman
[Scream like a wild fan.]

He's here *[wild scream]*!
I can't believe it *[louder wild scream]*!!
He's coming right this way *[even louder wild scream]*!!!
He's soooo handsome . . . and mysterious *[your loudest wild scream]*!!!!

With that, she began to faint . . . toward Zack, . . . but Zack caught her before she hit the ground. . . . For a moment, he thought about giving her CPR, . . . but just the thought of it caused the unconscious woman to scream hysterically, . . . until Zack dropped her to the ground. . . .

Next, a fisherman began to hop around the room, . . . ending up on center stage next to Zack as he sang his announcement to the tune of "Santa Claus Is Comin' to Town": . . .

Cue: Fisherman
[Sing to the tune of "Santa Claus Is Comin' to Town."]

You better not pout,
You better not cry,
You better not fret and I'm telling you why,
Jesus Christ is coming to town.

He knows when you've been sinful,
He knows when you've been real,
He knows when you take or give
So forgive and you'll be healed.

The man then let out a loud "Yahoo" . . . and jumped right in front of Zack so that Zack couldn't see a thing. . . . Zack tried jumping to his right, . . . then left, . . . then back, . . . and even forward, . . . but still he could not see.

Zack spied a tall sycamore tree that was beginning to move into view . . . —right up to center stage in fact. . . . Zack climbed up the tree and sat down. The tree had two long limbs that went up high, . . . and two that went really low, . . . so low that Zack could just see over the crowds. . . .

Just then Jesus came into view. . . . It seemed as if he were walking in slow motion, . . . waving to the crowds . . . and blowing kisses. . . . Seeing Jesus, the crowd went wild. . . . Then Jesus froze in his tracks, . . . and a hush fell over the crowd. . . . Jesus looked down at his feet, . . . causing everyone to stare at them too. . . . Slowly, Jesus wiggled his big toes, . . . then slowly raised his gaze upward . . . —even slower than that— . . . while the crowd followed along, . . . until their gaze fell upon Zack, the tax collector ("Boo! Hiss!"), . . . who was staring back at Jesus from the weakening sycamore tree. . . .

Jesus said to Zack in a voice like the President's: . . .

Cue: Jesus
[Speak like the President.]

Zacchaeus, did you know that I'm kind of partial to sinners and
    tax collectors, especially short Grinch-like *chief* tax collectors
    who like to climb trees?
So I'm wondering if you would be so kind
as to share dinner with me tonight? . . .
Let's say eightish at your house?
You bring the salad, and I'll bring the bread and wine.

This stunned the crowd, . . . which gasped in horror, . . . holding their collective breath . . . for a long time . . . —longer than most people thought they could— . . . until finally, all that trapped air just exploded at once, . . . causing Zack to fall out of the tree,

. . . knocking a lot of sense into him, . . . and giving the tree something to cheer about. . . . Zack hobbled over to Jesus and spoke to him in his most grown-up munchkin voice: . . .

> **Cue: Zaccheus**
> *[Speak in a munchkin voice.]*
>
> Master, you are greater than the Wizard of Oz!
> From now on, I'll only follow you down the yellow brick road.
> In fact, I'll give half of my gold to the poor.
> And the other half I'll use to buy a nice house in the country and . . .
> Uh, mmmmmm, oh, never mind. . . .
> I'll use that to pay back all the townsfolk I've cheated.

Jesus gave Zack a high five, . . . and the crowd went wild, . . . causing Zack to rise in stature, . . . and his heart to grow three times larger than the growth on the end of his nose!

The end.

Props

☐ a Bible with the reading marked
☐ signs displaying the boldfaced subheads for the commentaries

Reading and Commentaries

1. Invite someone to proclaim Luke 19:1–10.

2. After the reading, present the following commentaries to the group. Before you discuss each point, hand the sign displaying its subhead to the skit character it best applies to, and have that person stand in front of the group as you walk everyone through the meaning of the story.

The Town of Jericho

In today's world, Jericho would be considered a wealthy suburb of the big city of Jerusalem. It was located in the lush Jordan Valley and was a major crossroads for people coming and going to Jerusalem.

Taxes, Taxes, Taxes

Because of Jericho's wealth, the city was seen as a lucrative tax base for Rome. It was the tax collectors' job to make sure that Rome remained pleased with them by getting all the money Rome expected, which was sizeable enough. But on top of that, the tax collectors made their personal fortunes by collecting more than was due and keeping the remainder for themselves. This dishonesty and disregard for the rest of the working class made tax collectors one of the most hated groups of people in town, putting them in the same class as thieves and murderers.

Zacchaeus the Outcast

Zacchaeus was not only a tax collector, he was the *chief* tax collector, which brought him the most money . . . and the most disrespect. So great was the people's disgust for him and his kind that tax collectors were not allowed in the synagogue to worship. As it often is with people who are despised, anytime the townsfolk had a chance to show their disgust for him they would. Thus it was very likely to happen to this short man amid a large crowd. No doubt he got his share of kicks, spit, and taunts as he tried to catch a glimpse of Jesus, whom he hoped could see beyond his sinfulness.

Faith Climbing

Zacchaeus did not have much to lose in terms of the town's respect, so he must not have cared how silly he looked climbing that sycamore tree. He obviously would not let anything stand in his way in order to encounter Jesus. Perhaps it was taking this risk of faith that seemed to get Jesus's attention, along with a dinner invitation.

Repentance and Conversion

Of all the people in Jericho that day, Jesus chose the most despised to share dinner with. The stunned crowd could only gasp and mumble at Jesus's public commitment to dine with Zacchaeus. But the power of the invitation changed Zacchaeus. By raising up and recognizing the most hated in the town that day, Jesus gave Zacchaeus the dignity and respect he had longed for all of his life. Jesus's recognition of Zacchaeus set him free from the bondage of hatred and sin to which he had been shackled.

Payback Time

To prove to the town that he was a new man, Zacchaeus pledged to use half of his money to help the poor and to make restitution to those he had cheated over the years. This was good news to the whole town because restitution likely included everyone getting something, including the poor who had paid no taxes at all! What need did Zacchaeus have for money anyway? It had never brought him the dignity and respect that he had longed for all his life; only God's immense love that knows no boundaries could possibly have done that!

(The commentary notes are based on Robert Karris, editor, *The Collegeville Bible Commentary: New Testament,* page 970, and William Barclay, *Barclay's Daily Bible Study Series.*)

Props

☐ masking tape
☐ paper
☐ markers or pens, one for each person

Reflection and Discussion

1. Place two parallel strips of masking tape along the floor or wall, each about 10 feet long and about 10 inches apart from one another (see the diagram after step 3). Place a pile of paper on the floor along with the markers, and gather the group around the tape diagram.

2. Invite the participants to call out the names of different social classes or cliques that make up their world as teenagers today, and invite someone to write the name of each group or clique on one of the sheets of paper. For example, the young people might come up with social class groupings such as jocks, punks, geeks, teachers, parents, dropouts, and so on. Be sure only one name is listed per piece of paper and that no name used refers to more than one of the groups. Repeat this until all the various social classes or cliques that make up teens' lives have been listed.

3. Next, write the words "Top" and "Bottom" lengthwise on separate sheets of paper and place them at opposite ends of the sections of tape as shown in the following diagram:

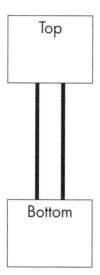

4. Redistribute the sheets of group names to participants around the circle (it does not matter who gets which name or that everyone receives one). Explain that the taped areas are the outside parts of the "Social Ladder of Modern Teens." The group's task is to establish who has the most power and respect within their teen culture today. This will require them to use the papers as rungs on a ladder in order to establish a societal "pecking order." Placing a sheet closer to the top of the ladder demonstrates that the group seems to have more power and respect than those below it.

5. Invite each person holding a paper to place it somewhere along the social ladder and to explain why she or he rated that group's power level as she or he did. If others in the group disagree with a particular placement, tell them that they will have their say once all the papers have been placed. If someone wants to place a paper next to another one, thereby giving it the same power rating, that is fine to do so as long as they offer an explanation as to why.

The ladder might resemble this diagram when done:

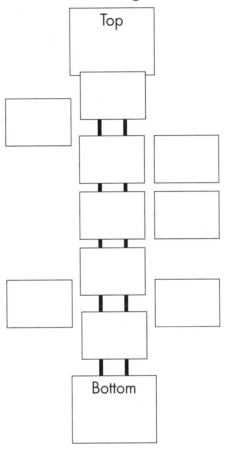

6. Once all the papers have been placed, invite some of the participants one at a time to come up to the ladder and reshuffle the order as they think it should be, explaining their reasoning with each move. Allow a few participants to do this, and then try to seek a general consensus as to what the teens' social ladder looks like. It does not really matter the particular order that ends up on the ladder or whether it's unanimous or not.

1. After completing the activity, ask the group to talk about the social ladder they built, using questions like the following:
- What kind of power do those near the top of the ladder possess? What does it look like? How does one attain it? Where does it come from?
- What is gained by being at the top of the ladder? at the bottom?
- How do the different "rungs" treat one another? In what direction is more respect shown? more disrespect? Why?

- Which group is made up of the largest number of people in your school? Which group is made up of the least? Why the difference?

2. Ask the group to imagine what Jesus would do if he came upon this social ladder today:
- Which groups would he find himself spending the most time with? How do you know this?
- What would he say to the groups at the top? the middle? the bottom?
- Where would Zacchaeus be found on this ladder?

3. Ask the participants to take a minute of quiet to think about where they find themselves on this ladder and how they feel about being there.

4. Conclude by switching the position of the signs that read "Top" and "Bottom" on the ladder and then saying:
- Jesus came to turn ladders (and our world) upside down—to free those imprisoned by the power of the social, political, and economic ladders of the day.
- Jesus consistently hung out on the "bottom rung," and by doing so directed a lot of attention and healing to folks who were hurting the most, whether physically, emotionally, or spiritually.
- Some brave people at the top of the ladder humbled themselves enough to let go and embrace this upside-down order, but many did not. These were the ones who wanted Jesus out of the picture; they wanted him to stop rocking the boat and turning their ladder, and their power, upside down.
- In the end, Jesus even turned death upside down by defeating it so we could all be freed from the prison bars of our human-made ladders. Zacchaeus discovered this freedom and it changed his life. So could you.

5. After a few minutes of silence, invite the participants who choose to do so to offer up a prayer to God out loud that begins with:
   Lord, help me to let go of . . .
   Then conclude by praying together the Lord's Prayer.

The Transfiguration

Produced by Luke 9: 28–36

Themes: Sacramental moments,
spiritual highs

Synopsis

This Scripture story uses the mountaintop moment of the Transfiguration to help the audience see the presence of God in the special moments of their lives and to examine how everyone is called to celebrate the spiritual highs through the daily practice of their faith.

Props

☐ a staff for Moses (This can be any stick, broom, or mop that is handy.)

☐ sunglasses, two pairs (optional)

Cast (9–10 people)

- ☐ Jesus (who speaks with an Italian accent)
- ☐ Peter (who speaks "surfer dude")
- ☐ James
- ☐ John
- ☐ Moses
- ☐ Elijah
- ☐ three to four people as the cloud (appoint one of the group as the "Voice of God")

If this is the first skit the group has done . . .

Explain that the characters selected are to do *exactly* what they hear the director read and are to be sure to face the audience during the performance. You should pause at each ellipsis (. . .) to give the characters time to do what you just read. When you come across a cue card, hold the book in front of the character who must read it, and point to the box containing the lines while emphasizing the voice in which it is to be read. Take your time and let the laughs roll!

Provide Moses and Elijah each with a pair of sunglasses or tell them to pantomime putting on a pair when cued to do so.

Skit

Jesus told Peter, James, and John to join hands and play a game of follow the leader behind him around the room. . . . When Jesus got back to center stage, he pointed up . . . —in the other direction— . . . to the top of a very large mountain, . . . and then said to them: . . .

Cue: Jesus
[Speak with an Italian accent.]
Last–a one-a up is a Pharisee-a.

They each began to run . . . in place, . . . but after a little while they started to breathe heavier . . . and deeper . . . and then began to crawl . . . in place. . . . Soon the disciples started asking Jesus lots of questions about where they were headed . . .

and what was for dinner . . . and who was supposed to bring the popcorn. . . . Finally Peter asked in his surfer dude voice: . . .

> **Cue: Peter**
> *[Speak like a surfer dude.]*
>
> Dude, are we *there* yet?!

Jesus turned around, . . . slowly, . . . and thought about that question for a long time, . . . pondering its significance . . . and questioning its ponderance . . . and finally responding thoughtfully with: . . .

> **Cue: Jesus**
> *[Speak with an Italian accent.]*
>
> No-a, not-a yet-a.

The group then took one big hop, . . . two small skips, . . . and 3.14 jumps, . . . as the four arrived at the top of the mountain with a thud. . . . Peter, James, and John were so tired from the climb that they fell against each other . . . —the other way— . . . and nodded off to sleep, . . . making snoring sounds like a group of giggling children.

Suddenly Moses leapt onstage, appearing to the right of Jesus. . . . Moses held his staff in one hand . . . —the other one— . . . and had an eager look on his face. . . . Next, Elijah, the great prophet, twirled onstage, . . . ending up on Jesus's left side with both fingers pointing at Jesus as both exclaimed in unison: . . .

> **Cue: Moses and Elijah**
>
> You da man, Jesus!

Upon hearing this, Jesus did the moonwalk across the stage . . . and spun around . . . twice. . . . Then his clothes became so bright that Moses and Elijah had to put on sunglasses. . . . The light startled Peter, James, and John awake. . . . They rubbed their eyes in disbelief . . . and then rubbed each other's eyes. . . . The sight before them was so unbelievable that the three bowed down to Jesus crying out, "We're not worthy" over and over again.

Then everything froze, . . . as a cloud swirled and descended onto the scene, . . . circling Jesus . . . —in the other direction. . . . A voice called out from the cloud: . . .

> **Cue: Voice of God**
> *[Speak slowly, deeply, and with power.]*
>
> This is my beloved son, the main man!
> Listen to him . . .
> Or else!

With that, the cloud made a loud thundering noise, . . . followed by the sound of rushing wind, . . . and then flew off to the east, . . . then circled back west, . . . finally deciding to be seated in the audience. . . .

The disciples were so impressed by all this that they started clapping in unison and performed a cheer: . . .

> **Cue: Three Disciples**
> *[Use cheerleader voices and rhythms.]*
>
> Hey, Jesus, you're so fine.
> You're so fine I'll call you mine.
> Hey, Jesus!
> Hey, Jesus!
> Wooohoooo *[Do big cheers and jumps.]*

As James and John began to do the splits, . . . Peter leaped forward and said to James and John: . . .

Cue: Peter
[Speak like a surfer dude.]

Dude, that was so totally, outrageously awesome!
We should set up three megatents
And get the rest of the dudes up here for a bodacious party!
Maybe we could even make this into a super secret club
With cool handshakes, funky cheers, and gnarly decoder rings!
And James, Dude, pleeeaaase don't forget the popcorn this time.

Just as Peter finished saying these words, Moses and Elijah vanished from sight in a double poof, . . . causing the whole audience to chant, "We're not worthy" over and over again. . . .

Then Jesus did the moonwalk around the disciples, . . . ending up in front of them, . . . pointing back down the mountain. . . . Then he said: . . .

Cue: Jesus
[Speak with an Italian accent.]

I know-a you guys-a like-a to cheer-a and eat-a the popcorn-a,
But-a we have-a some more hiking to do-a, and it ends up-a in-a Jerusalem-a.
And along-a the way-a, we've got some-a healing
And teaching-a to do-a, so let's get going, huh?

With that, Jesus made the three disciples play a game of follow the leader . . . as they went down the mountain . . . and back into the audience. . . .

The end.

Props

☐ a Bible with the reading marked
☐ signs displaying the boldfaced subheads for the commentaries

Reading and Commentaries

1. Invite someone to proclaim Luke 9:28–36.

2. After the reading, present the following commentaries to the group. Before you discuss each point, hand the sign displaying its subhead to the skit character it best applies to, and have that person stand in front of the group as you walk everyone through the meaning of the story.

On the Way to the Cross

Jesus and the disciples are on their way to Jerusalem, where Jesus will be crucified. He has already forewarned his followers of his looming death and the Resurrection to follow, but they don't seem to grasp its possibility. The Transfiguration story serves as both a reminder to the disciples (and the reader) of who Jesus is as well as a momentary retreat to get recharged for the difficult journey that awaits them down the mountain.

Getting Close to God

Mountains symbolize being close to or next to God. Many significant events in Jewish history occurred on mountains, such as Moses meeting God in the burning bush and Jesus's Sermon on the Mount. The event of the Transfiguration is no exception. The cloud from which the voice of God is heard is also a symbol of the presence of God in that moment.

Jesus: Fulfillment of the Law and the Prophets

Moses is known by all as the great lawgiver—the one to whom God presented the Law (through the Ten Commandments) atop a mountain two thousand years earlier. Elijah is considered the greatest Hebrew prophet. The fact that both appear next to Jesus affirms that Jesus is the fulfillment of both the Law and of all that the prophets had promised. To top it off, the voice of God affirms Jesus as his chosen Son and then instructs the disciples and all of us to "listen to him" (verse 35).

Wanting to Stay

Upon seeing this amazing sight, Peter does what most of us would do. He wants to set up some tents and stay awhile in order to bask in the glory that is present in this awesome moment. It's a once-in-a-lifetime occurrence that will never be repeated. Like Peter, we have the same human desire to hang on to these types of moments for as long as we can, even searching out additional ones so that we might re-experience that spiritual high.

The Journey Down

Jesus knows where the road ahead leads (to Jerusalem and the cross). He resists the temptation to stick around and recall the good times, and leads Peter, James, and John back down the mountain in order to continue the ministry he was sent to do, a ministry that is leading him ever more closely to his death and Resurrection. In Luke's Gospel, the first thing that Jesus does *after* the Transfiguration is to heal a boy possessed by a demon. Jesus wants to show his followers that discipleship is lived out in the plains and valleys of day-to-day life, not just in those special mountaintop moments that come our way from time to time.

(The commentary notes are based on Robert Karris, editor, *The Collegeville Bible Commentary*, pages 954–955, and William Barclay, *Barclay's Daily Bible Study Series*.)

Props

☐ a candle and a lighter or matches
☐ a tape or CD of reflective instrumental music and a tape or CD player (optional)
☐ scrap paper and pens, one of each for each person

Reflection and Discussion

1. Lower the lights and light a candle to set the tone for the sharing that is about to take place. You may also want to play some soft instrumental music to make the moment more reflective and focused. Distribute scrap paper and pens to the participants.

2. Tell the group that the Transfiguration was a special moment in which the disciples had a front-row seat to the glory and grace of God. Invite the participants to think about a time when they were witnesses to a transfiguring moment, a time when they felt very close to God or could easily see God's presence at work within them or around them. Tell them to jot their idea on their scrap paper.

3. Place the candle in front of you as you share a mountaintop moment experience of God from your own life with the group (a time when you felt really close to God). Be sure to include the setting you were in (on a retreat, hiking a scenic path, experiencing Reconciliation, and so forth).

4. Now place the candle in front of someone in the group and invite them to share their mountaintop moment. If they do not wish to, tell them they may pass (and be returned to later if they wish), but no matter what they choose (whether to share a story or pass), they must place the candle in front of another person and invite him or her to share their story. Continue this mutual invitation process until all have shared and all who passed have been re-invited to share (they may choose to pass again if they wish).

CURTAIN call

1. Lead the group in a discussion of the following questions:
- What makes it easier to see God in special moments and harder to see God in ordinary times?
- Are we tempted to become a "mountaintop junkie"—to go from spiritual high to spiritual high without ever coming down the mountain?
- Why does Jesus want us to come down the mountain and not stay up there?
- What road is God asking you to walk in this coming week? Why?

2. After a few minutes of silence, invite the young people to conclude with a petition of thanksgiving for whatever they wish at this time. Conclude by praying together the Glory Be.

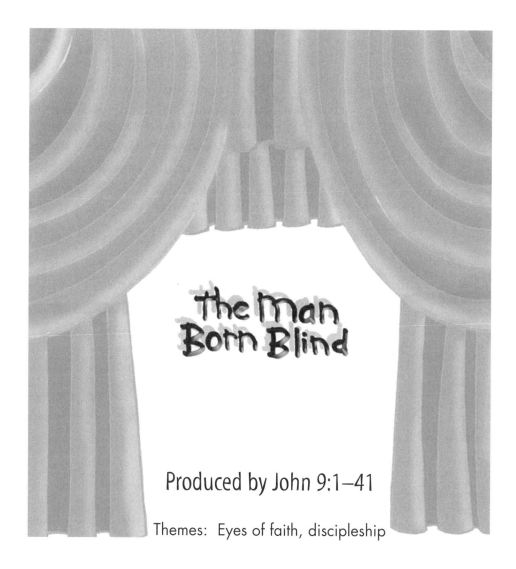

the Man Born Blind

Produced by John 9:1–41

Themes: Eyes of faith, discipleship

Synopsis

This Scripture story invites the audience to walk the journey of faith with the man born blind in order to examine what enlightens and what distorts one's ability to see God alive and active in the present moment.

Cast (8–9 people plus the audience)

☐ a man born blind (who speaks with a Southern drawl)
☐ Jesus (who speaks like a game show host)
☐ two or three disciples
☐ two parents (a mother and a father)
☐ two Pharisees (a tall one who speaks like a bad cop and a shorter one who speaks like a good cop)
☐ the audience

If this is the first skit the group has done . . .

Explain that the characters selected are to do *exactly* what they hear the director read and are to be sure to face the audience during the performance. You should pause at each ellipsis (. . .) to give the characters time to do what you just read. When you come across a cue card, hold the book in front of the character who must read it, and point to the box containing the lines while emphasizing the voice in which it is to be read. Take your time and let the laughs roll!

During the skit, the audience will be instructed to do various things, which they are asked to do when they hear it announced in the script.

The people playing the Pharisees will be instructed to keep their hands over their eyes as if they are peering through binoculars the whole time. Do not allow them to take their hands away from their eyes during the skit. If they do, remind them to keep their hands up around their eyes.

Skit

Jesus and his disciples were dancing their way through town, . . . when they saw a blind man who was feeling his way around . . . and begging for money. . . . So Jesus decided to play a game with his disciples. . . . Speaking like a game show host, he said: . . .

Cue: Jesus
[Speak like a game show host.]
Welcome to *Seeing Is Believing,* the show where
what you see is exactly what you get!
Our first toss-up question is:
Why is this man blind? Is it because . . .
A. He sinned so bad, God is punishing him.
B. His parents sinned so bad that God is punishing him.
C. He forgot to open his eyes this morning.
D. This is a trick question.

The disciples huddled together to figure out the answer. . . . Soon they found themselves arguing about who the smartest was, . . . agreeing that it must be . . . Then they argued about who smelled the worst, . . . finally agreeing and pointing at . . . Then they remembered that they were on a game show watched by millions of people around Palestine, . . . so together they shouted out their answer. . . .

Jesus invited them forward to see the prize they would get. . . . As they leaned over Jesus's shoulder . . . —the other one— . . . he spit into his hands, . . . then gathered up some dirt, . . . and began making a mud cake, . . . which he took to the blind man, placing it on his eyes. . . . This really grossed out the disciples . . . and the audience. . . . Then Jesus said to the blind man: . . .

Cue: Jesus
[Speak like a game show host.]

Congratulations, you are today's winner on *Seeing Is Believing*. All you have to do to claim your prize is wash off your face.

But the blind man protested, . . . saying that he had just bathed last month. . . . But even the audience cheered the man on to *please* accept his prize. . . . Jesus said to him: . . .

Cue: Jesus
[Speak like a game show host.]

If you could only see what I see
Then you'd see that which we all see
When we see you which is that you need to see your way
   to the bath
As soon as possible.

With that, Jesus splashed some water on the man and stepped offstage as the blind man responded in a Southern drawl: . . .

Cue: Blind Man
[Speak with a southern drawl.]

I guess I see what you mean about that bath,
I'm all caked in mud!
Hey, wait a second. . . .
If I'm blind, how can I read this cue card?
Or see this audience in front of me?

The audience shouted, "It's a miracle," . . . and a few people in the front row jumped up . . . and picked up the blind man . . . and carried him over to the Pharisees, . . . who were always looking through their hands as if they were holding binoculars . . . that they never put down, no matter what. . . . The people carrying the Man Formerly Known as the Blind Man set him down in front of the Pharisees, . . . which caused the Pharisees to twirl around and bump into each other. . . . With their hands still encircling their eyes, the Pharisees began their interrogation, with the tall one playing the role of the bad cop, and the short one playing the role of the good cop: . . .

Cue: Tall Pharisee
[Speak like an angry "bad cop."]

How say can you see by the dawn's early light?
And on the Sabbath of all days! Well? What say you?
What's the matter, don't you see me talking to you?
You want a piece of these binoculars?!
Well, what are you waiting for, c'mon!

Cue: Short Pharisee
[Speak like a kinder "good cop."]

So Former Blind Man, who helped you to see like this?
Just tell us so we can bring him in here
For the recognition he so justly deserves.

But the Man Formerly Known as the Blind Man could only shake his head . . . and shrug his shoulders . . . and scratch his ear . . . —the other one— . . . and smirk, . . . really big, . . . because he had never seen the man who cured him. This made both the Pharisees so mad that they stomped their feet . . . and huffed . . . and puffed . . . and roared out: . . .

> **Cue: Short and Tall Pharisees**
> *[Speak loudly and in an angry tone.]*
>
> Bring in the sinner's parents!

Just then the parents raced in, . . . but were unable to stop and ran right into the Pharisees, . . . who tumbled to the ground, still holding their hands over their eyes. . . . After getting up (without using their hands), they demanded to know if the man had been blind from birth or if they were secretly on Extreme Makeover. . . . The parents were so afraid of the Pharisees that they shook in their boots . . . and bit their nails, . . . then bit each other's nails. . . . Finally they managed to mumble something unintelligible . . . and then groaned loudly . . . and then tried to bite the Pharisees' nails. . . .

This made the Pharisees roar with anger, . . . so they leaped in front of the Man Formerly Known as the Blind Man, . . . while the taller one said:

> **Cue: Tall Pharisee**
> *[Speak like an angry "bad cop."]*
>
> We happen to know that the man who did this is not only a sinner,
> But he slurps his soup.
> Agree with us and you will be allowed to see
> The next showing of *The Ten Commandments* for free!

This made the Man Formerly Known as the Blind Man yawn . . . because he heard the movie went on forever and was shown every Passover anyway. So he said to the Pharisees: . . .

Cue: Blind Man
[Speak with a Southern drawl.]

Why don't you two just give it up for God, huh?
You stand there with your fancy, shmancy binoculars,
Thinking that you know and see everything,
But the guy who did this is no ordinary guy.
And you're mad because you can't see that.
So tell me, who's the blind one now, huh?.

With that, the Pharisees ordered the former blind man's parents to pick him up . . . and toss him out of the Temple, . . . causing him to land in front of Jesus. . . . Upon seeing Jesus, the man immediately began worshiping him. . . . Jesus then said to the audience: . . .

Cue: Jesus
[Speak like a game show host.]

I came to bring a little light into the world so you could see better.
But some, it seems, *[Turn and glare at the Pharisees.]*
Like to be kept in the dark because they can't handle the Light.

This caused the Pharisees to spin around, . . . bumping into each other and losing their binoculars in the mud for good. . . .

The end.

Props

☐ a Bible with the reading marked
☐ signs displaying the boldfaced subheads for the commentaries

Reading and Commentaries

1. Invite someone to proclaim John 9:1–41.

2. After the reading, present the following commentaries to the group. Before you discuss each point, hand the sign displaying its subhead to the skit character it best applies to, and have that person stand in front of the group as you walk everyone through the meaning of the story.

A Metaphor for Faith

The story of the man born blind is found only in the Gospel of John and is a wonderful symbol for the whole faith community of how an individual might come to first discover, then uncover, the presence of God in the here and now. Although it is a long reading, it presents itself as an unfolding drama that had much meaning for the early Christians for whom John's Gospel was written.

Blind Sinners

It was a popular notion during Jesus's day that people with disabilities (blindness, deafness, muteness) and illnesses (leprosy, hemorrhages, seizures) were "cursed" by God, either for sins they had committed or for sins that their parents or grandparents had committed. These unfortunate people were looked down upon and judged by others as unworthy sinners. The fact that the man in this story had been blind from birth indicated a distorted belief that he was being judged harshly by both God and the religious leaders for the sins of his predecessors.

Washing in the Waters of Siloam

Jesus instructs the man to go and wash in a public pool known as Siloam, meaning "the one who has been sent." This ritual washing that brings about the man's sight is symbolic of the sacrament of Baptism, in which the blessed waters bring about a spiritual rebirth and, with it, a new way of seeing and being in the world. From the moment the man washes away the mud, he is a new man, just as we are new creations after our Baptism.

Fear and Unbelief

One would think that such a miracle would bring about great rejoicing, but instead it only stirs things up within the former blind man's family and with the Pharisees, the religious leaders of the day.

The parents do not want to speak on their son's behalf because they are afraid to be thrown out of the Temple. When John's Gospel was written, Rome acknowledged only the Jewish faith as an authorized or protected one. To be thrown out of the Temple was equivalent to a death sentence, which is why the parents were so afraid to speak on their son's behalf.

Healing on the Sabbath

The Pharisees are threatened by this miracle and by Jesus because he does what they cannot, namely to help people see God's grace and light at work in the world. Because Jesus makes mud and cures on the Sabbath (both of which were forbidden by Jewish Law), they hope to get the blind man to publicly denounce Jesus as a sinner who could not possibly do what the man is claiming.

From Seeing to Believing

As the story unfolds, the man journeys from total darkness (spiritual blindness) to seeing (acknowledging God) to believing (total commitment to God). In the end, he stands up to the Pharisees and proclaims Jesus as the One who has been sent by God (similar to the meaning of the name of Siloam) and pays the price for this admission by being tossed out of the Temple. This unfolding journey of faith mirrors our own faith journey. We are brought up to see and to learn about God, but at some point we must claim that vision as our own and then act upon it. This is the big step in discipleship, when we, like the man born blind, take the risk of faith and stand up for who and whose we are, no matter what the cost involved.

The Upside-Down Message

Jesus ends this story by speaking to the Pharisees about blindness and sight, letting them know that their insistence on being in control and in controlling others with the Law only serves to blind them further from the Truth that is standing before them. Once again, Jesus demonstrates an upside-down Kingdom where the blind can see and the sighted are made blind, where sinners are raised up and those who judge the sinners are brought low. No wonder they call this stuff Good News!

(The commentary notes are drawn from Robert Karris, editor, *The Collegeville Bible Commentary: New Testament*, pages 995–998, and William Barclay, *Barclay's Daily Bible Study Series*.)

Props

☐ newsprint
☐ markers, one for each person

Reflection and Discussion

1. Divide the young people into small groups of four, and give two sheets of newsprint and four markers to each group. Direct each group to draw one large eye on each sheet of newsprint. The eye should be just a basic outline drawing with little detail because people will be writing on the inside of the eye. Ask each group to label one of the eye drawings, "Enlightened" and the other one "Distorted."

2. Tell the groups to work first on their distorted eye image by filling in words or images of things that tend to blind today's young people to seeing God in the midst of life, such as media images that use women as objects, or the pursuit to be number one no matter what. Be sure to encourage everyone in the small groups to write or draw things inside or around the eye that fit into this category.

3. Repeat this process with the enlightened eye, but this time invite the groups to draw images or words that lead young people today to seeing God in the present moment, such as going on a retreat or taking time to talk with a friend who's struggling.

4. When all the groups are done, invite them to hang all the enlightened eyes together on the wall (or place them together on the floor) and then place all the distorted eyes together. Invite each group to share some of the more significant things on their sheets that enlighten and distort our ability to see God at work in the world today.

curtain call

1. Lead the group in a discussion of the following questions:

- Of all the things that distort young peoples' belief in God, which is the most severe in your opinion? Why?
- Of all the things that enlighten young peoples' belief in God, which is the most helpful in your opinion? Why?
- Where can the majority of distortions that are listed be found? Why do they exist in such multitude there? What would it take for someone with "distorted vision" to become enlightened and able to see God?
- Of all the distortions listed, which are you most susceptible to? Which gift of sight from the enlightened list do you most possess? Which do you most need right now?

2. After a couple of minutes of silence, dim the lights (if it's not possible, then have the participants close their eyes). Then reread the last part of the Gospel story (John 9:35–41) and invite each person to respond to the following unfinished prayer sentence out loud if they wish to:

Lord, help me to see . . .

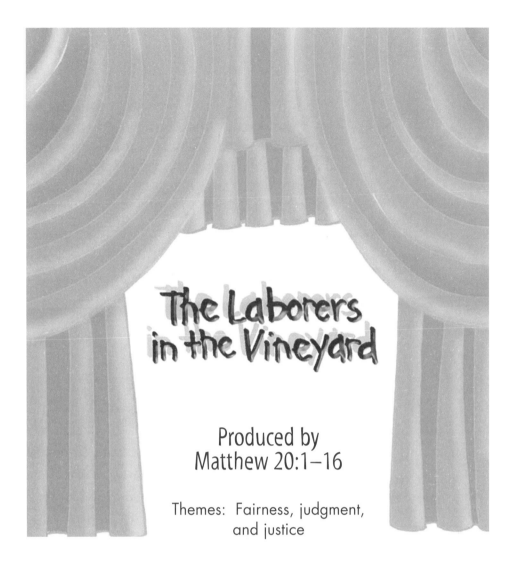

The Laborers in the Vineyard

Produced by
Matthew 20:1–16

Themes: Fairness, judgment, and justice

Synopsis

This Scripture story uses the parable of the laborers in the vineyard to help the audience understand the all-encompassing and inclusive nature of God's invitation to become a disciple, no matter when the invitation is responded to. This is challenging to our own sense of fairness and justice.

Cast (6 people plus the audience)

☐ five workers (the tallest speaks like Cookie Monster)
☐ store owner (who speaks proper English)
☐ the audience

If this is the first skit the group has done . . .
Explain that the characters selected are to do *exactly* what they hear the director read and are to be sure to face the audience during the performance. You should pause at each ellipsis (. . .) to give the characters time to do what you just read. When you come across a cue card, hold the book in front of the character who must read it, and point to the box containing the lines while emphasizing the voice in which it is to be read. Take your time and let the laughs roll!

During the skit, the audience will be instructed to do various things, which they are asked to do when they hear it announced in the script.

Skit

A group of workers were in the marketplace playing freeze tag with the best-looking one being it, . . . when a wealthy store owner strolled up to them. . . . The store owner sized up each worker . . . and asked the tallest among them to show him how strong he was . . . by picking up the person next to him . . . while tap dancing to the tune of "Twinkle, Twinkle Little Star," . . . which was sung by the person he was holding. . . . The store owner then announced in the voice of a proper Englishman: . . .

Cue: Store Owner
[Speak in a proper English voice.]

I say, old chap, you are quite strong,
And you certainly can carry a tune *[ha, ha, ha]*!
How about we strike a deal . . .
You work in my store today and I'll pay you a jolly-good rate at
    day's end?
Do we have an agreement, then?

The tallest worker clapped his hands . . . and shook his head in agreement . . . —faster— . . . because he had a family of ten to feed. . . . He pointed to them in the audience. . . . The store owner asked him to stand in one of the corners of the room and sing the "YMCA" song refrain using full hand motions until he was asked to stop. . . .

The store owner was so pleased by this performance that he jumped up . . . and did a little jig onstage. . . . Turning to the two next tallest workers, . . . he asked them if they would like a day's wages of work. . . . They both jumped up and down . . . and did a cheerleader leap and yell. . . . The owner sent these two to another corner of the room to sing and play pat-a-cake until instructed to stop. . . . The audience gave the three performers a standing ovation. . . . This pleased the store owner so much that he turned to the next tallest worker on stage . . . and asked the person to tiptoe to a vacant corner of the room . . . and do a hula dance until asked to stop. . . .

The audience loved this new act so much that they gave high fives to those around them. . . . The owner turned to the last worker remaining, . . . who could only fidget back and forth because he had to go . . . really bad. . . . The owner knew there was one more corner of the room remaining, so he pointed in that direction and asked the worker to waddle over to it . . . and do some disco dance moves until told to stop. . . . Soon after the worker started, . . . the owner realized the mistake he had made and loudly yelled "Stop!" . . . freezing the workers in mid-movement.

The owner called all the workers back to center stage . . . and, beginning with the shortest, . . . gave the person a big hug, . . . followed by a huge handshake . . . and then twirled the person around . . . three times. . . . The owner repeated this same movement with the hula dancer . . . as well as the pat-a-cake team. . . . Finally the owner spun around to face the "YMCA" performer, . . . who said in a voice sounding like Cookie Monster from *Sesame Street:* . . .

Cue: Tallest Worker
[Speak in a Cookie Monster voice.]

Oh boy, it's my turn!
Can't wait to see what I get since me dance all day long.
Maybe special surprise in store for me?

Then the store owner stood before the "YMCA" performer and gave him a big hug, . . . followed by a huge handshake . . . and then twirled him around three times . . . and then stopped! The worker was startled, . . . surprised, . . . and angry, . . . saying: . . .

Cue: Tallest Worker
[Speak in a Cookie Monster voice.]

Me work all day for you.
You pay me same as those others who not work as long.
What deal here, you not like to stay at the YMCA?

The store owner took the worker by the shoulders . . . and looked straight into his eyes to say: . . .

Cue: Store Owner
[Speak in a proper English voice.]

My dear fellow,
You mustn't think that way.
Did we not have a proper agreement to pay you a day's wages?
Well, then, I've chosen to do the same with each of you.
Do you fault me for being a generous chap?
I say, that's not yours to judge, now is it?
So before you tally on, would you be so kind as to remember this:
In my store, the last shall be first
And the first shall be last!

And the audience all cheered, "Jolly good show"! . . .

The end.

Props

☐ a Bible with the reading marked
☐ signs displaying the boldfaced subheads for the commentaries

Reading and Commentaries

1. Invite someone to proclaim Matthew 20:1–16.

2. After the reading, present the following commentaries to the group. Before you discuss each point, hand the sign displaying its subhead to the skit character it best applies to, and have that person stand in front of the group as you walk everyone through the meaning of the story.

The Marketplace Employment Line

When people in Jesus's day wanted to hire help, they would go to the marketplace, where those seeking work for the day would stand in line, waiting in hope that they would be selected for the next job. The day laborers who gathered there lived day by day, hand-to-mouth because a day's wages (a drachma) was just enough to get their family through until the next day's job came along. Several days of unemployment meant that families would go hungry.

The Need for Speed

Those listening to Jesus tell this parable were not surprised that people were being hired even with just a few hours left in the day. During harvesttime, laborers were in high demand because the window of opportunity to harvest the crop was always a short-lived one. A full day's work consisted of a twelve-hour day stretching from sunrise (6 a.m.) until sundown (6 p.m.), and the landowner wanted as many people as possible working his land during that time so that the crop could be harvested at its peak to bring the best price and to keep it from spoiling in the fields. This required landowners to hire people whenever help was available, even if it was midday or later, because an hour or two of extra hands could mean the difference between profit and loss. What did surprise the listeners of the parable was what each ended up being paid.

And Justice for All

The parable speaks not only of God's sense of fairness and justice, a true "justice for all," it also sends a clear message to all people that there is no time like the present to turn toward God and follow God. Whether you have accepted and believed in God since the earliest of years, experienced a change of heart during midlife or even later, God offers the same reward to all who come to him openly and honestly—namely an eternal life and love in God's Kingdom. As the saying goes, "It just doesn't get any better than this!"

Reversal of Fortunes and Status

Matthew places this parable following the story of Jesus blessing the children, in which Jesus challenges the adults to become more like children, and the story of the rich young man who went away sad because he could not let go of the wealth he had. The story that follows this parable has the mother of James and John begging Jesus to let her sons have a place of prominence in the Kingdom of God, and Jesus replying that those who wish to be great must serve others. Each of these stories upholds the truth found in the parable of the laborers: that the Kingdom of God is an upside-down one in which the rich are made powerless, the poor and childlike become the first in line, and "the last will be first and the first will be last!" (verse 16). Each of these stories underscores the Good News that the great Kingdom of God is open to all.

A Wide-Eyed God of Justice

Matthew's Gospel was written for a Jewish audience, many of whom saw themselves as the only ones deserving of God's justice. Many Jews felt that Gentiles (nonbelievers) could not be accepted into the Kingdom of God. This parable spoke clearly and powerfully to God's inclusiveness rather than exclusiveness, giving both Jews and non-Jews the Good News that God's idea of fairness and justice is a wide-eyed, all-encompassing one that is never too late to take advantage of.

(The commentary notes are based on Robert Karris, editor, *The Collegeville Bible Commentary: New Testament*, page 890, and William Barclay, *Barclay's Daily Bible Study Series*.)

Props

☐ tape
☐ four signs that read:
- Very Fair
- Somewhat Fair
- Somewhat Unfair
- Totally Unfair

Reflection and Discussion

1. Place the signs in different areas of the room or floor (such as one per wall or corner). Tell the group that you will read a scenario and that when you are done, each person is to go and stand by the sign that best describes how fair they feel the situation was *without saying anything out loud.*

2. Read part A of the scenario (listed following step 3) and allow the participants to move to their chosen location in the room. After everyone has taken a stand, go from sign to sign and invite those who want to comment on why they chose that particular sign to do so.

3. After everyone comments on part A of the scenario, read part B (the "rest of the story") and invite those who wish to move to a new sign to do so. Then invite those who moved to say why they did. Complete each of the scenarios in the same manner (or as many as time allows).

Scenario 1: Concert tickets

Part A. One of your favorite bands is coming to your town for a one-night concert. You wait in line for five hours to get the best seats for you and two of your friends. There is a ten-ticket maximum for any one person. With just a few more people to go, the woman in front of you makes a few phone calls and in five minutes, ten other people join her in line, and each of them purchases ten tickets. When you get to the window, the seats you were hoping to get are now sold out, requiring you to get seats in the "nosebleed" section. How fair is this?

Note to leader: Do not read Part B until after part A has been discussed by the group.

Part B. The person in front of you was a volunteer for the Make-a-Wish Foundation who was trying to fulfill the wishes of terminally ill teenagers who wanted to attend this concert. The people she called were other volunteers who left their jobs to come and purchase the tickets for the terminally ill teens who wanted to attend the concert. How fair is this?

Scenario 2: Stolen property

Part A. A store owner in a poor section of town has caught a man stealing from his store so he calls the police. He presses charges to send a message to the rest of the community that anyone stealing in his store will be prosecuted. During the trial, the judge, noting that it was the defendant's first offense, lets him off with just a warning, without even a fine, and the store owner leaves the courtroom having to listen to the cheers of the guilty man's family and friends. How fair is this?

Note to leader: Do not read Part B until after part A has been discussed by the group.

Part B. The defendant had been laid off work after a serious illness. His family was out of food and money, and he had gone to the store to steal some bread and canned vegetables to feed his family. The judge, upon hearing his story, imposes no fine or jail time and refers the family to social services to get the assistance they need. How fair is this?

Scenario 3: Out of a job

Part A. You apply for a summer job at a local grocery store. You know the final decision is between you and one other person who goes to your school. The other person is generally regarded as a troublemaker, and you've heard that his older brothers have already been involved in criminal activity; one of them is even in jail for killing someone. You appear to be a lock for the job, but when the manager calls, he says that even though you were an excellent candidate, he has selected the other person. How fair is this?

Note to leader: Do not read Part B until after part A has been discussed by the group.

Part B. During the job interview, the applicant broke down and told the manager that this job was his last hope of getting away from the gang that had been "recruiting" him, the same gang that his brothers had gotten involved in and the one that led his oldest brother into taking another's life. The applicant was hoping to get into a small college at the end of the summer, but he needed to save enough money to make a break from the life that was waiting for him. The manager, having been down a similar road years before, agreed to help the applicant out for the summer by giving him the job. How fair is this?

1. Lead the group in a discussion of the following questions:

- What makes things unfair? Why did hearing the rest of the story help change some people's minds about what's unfair and what's not?
- What causes people to judge others so quickly or to see life as treating them unfairly? What do people gain by doing that? What do people lose?
- How often do we really know the "full story" of someone before we pass judgment on them? Has that ever happened to you?
- How does the parable of the laborers in the vineyard speak to the scenarios we just discussed? Which of the laborers do you relate to the most? Why?
- Our court system says it practices "blind justice," but Christians believe that God practices "wide-eyed justice," a judgment that sees, knows, and understands the whole story of every person. Which would you rather have judging you and your life? Why?
- How does this Scripture parable challenge your sense of fairness, faith, privilege, and justice?

2. Invite the group to close the discussion by spending a few minutes in silence thinking about a person or situation that they have been judging unfairly and that they would like to ask God's help in letting go of.

After a few minutes, invite the group to join hands and pray together the Lord's Prayer, instructing the group to pause for five seconds after the lines: "forgive us our trespasses" and again after saying "as we forgive those who trespass against us."

The Rich Man and Lazarus

Produced by Luke 16:19–31

Themes: Eternal life,
misuse of wealth

Synopsis

This Scripture story invites the audience to reflect on the parable of the rich man and Lazarus by considering the different voices that call out to us to notice the needs and concerns of those around us and to respond to them as Christ would.

Props

☐ a chair in the middle of the "stage" area
☐ a handkerchief for the rich man (This could be a napkin, a piece of cloth, or even a sock.)

Cast (9 people plus the audience)

☐ the rich man (who speaks like Elmer Fudd)
☐ Hades, the pet dog
☐ a servant (who speaks like a refined butler)
☐ Lazarus

☐ Abraham (who speaks in a boring monotone voice)
☐ two angels
☐ two devils named Fire and Brimstone
☐ the audience

If this is the first skit the group has done . . .
Explain that the characters selected are to do *exactly* what they hear the director read and are to be sure to face the audience during the performance. You should pause at each ellipsis (. . .) to give the characters time to do what you just read. When you come across a cue card, hold the book in front of the character who must read it, and point to the box containing the lines while emphasizing the voice in which it is to be read. Take your time and let the laughs roll!

During the skit, the audience will be instructed to do various things, which they should do when they hear it announced in the script.

Skit

The rich man walked onstage with his pet dog, Hades, prancing by his side, . . . then skidding to a halt, . . . so that the man could take a moment to admire his expensive rings, . . . sweetly kissing all of them. . . . He had one on each finger . . . —of both hands. . . . Then he and Hades sashayed over to the chair at center stage. . . . The man took out his hankie . . . and delicately dusted off the seat . . . before carefully seating himself in his chair, . . . crossing his right leg over his left, . . . and ordering Hades to sit, . . . lie down, . . . and roll over. . . . Then he called for his servant . . . by yodeling. . . .

Immediately the servant rushed over to the rich man and knelt down to kiss one of his rings . . . —on the other hand— . . . but could not decide which one to kiss, so he just shook his hand daintily, . . . while petting the dog on the head and fluffing up its hair. . . . Then the servant looked at the audience . . . and gagged. . . . Turning to the rich man, the servant said, in a very refined butler's voice: . . .

Cue: Servant
[Speak like a refined butler.]

Master, your dinner is ready.
Tonight we are featuring a lightly baked shrimp,
    stuffed with crabmeat and served over a zesty bed
    of flavored rice topped with an exquisite sherry sauce
    that is to die for.

The rich man smacked his lips while the dog drooled on himself.
. . . Then the rich man clapped his hands together . . .
—twice— . . . and ordered his meal brought to him posthaste, .
. . which the butler did forthwith. . . .

As the butler began feeding the rich man his shrimp, . . . one at a
time, . . . a poor beggar named Lazarus began to drag himself
toward center stage, . . . slowly, . . . painfully, . . . moaning
with every movement . . . because of all the oozing, leaking,
rotting, infected sores that covered his arms . . . and legs . . .
and ears . . . and face . . . and both big toes. . . . As soon
as the dog saw this, he hopped over to Lazarus to lick the sores on
his big toe, . . . but the rich man yodeled angrily, . . . and the
dog yelped in terror . . . and ran back to the rich man, . . .
who looked at Lazarus with pity, . . . followed by nausea, . . .
and then ordered the servants to give the leftovers to the dog. . . .
Hades licked the plate clean, . . . leaving Lazarus to groan and
moan even louder, . . . before he clutched his throat, . . . then
his big toe . . . —the other one— . . . and finally his left elbow,
. . . whereupon Lazarus rolled over . . . —the other way—
. . . and died, . . . as the audience sighed. . . .

Just then the rich man stood up with a look of horror, . . . followed
by a gasp, . . . as he clutched his chest, . . . toppling over
toward the servant, . . . who wasn't looking and missed catching
him, . . . causing the rich man to fall down on the floor . . .
dead. . . .

Hades and the servant gasped, . . . grieved, . . . comforted each other, . . . dragged the rich man over to Lazarus, . . . took the rich man's money . . . and the remaining food, . . . and leaped offstage. . . .

Then two angels entered with Abraham. . . . The angels were flitting and flying about. . . . Abraham stood by the chair and peered at the two dead men lying side by side. . . . He ordered the angels to give one a lift, . . . so they flew over and picked up Lazarus and lovingly . . . and compassionately . . . set him onto the chair, as Abraham and the angels breathed on him . . . —harder— . . . bringing Lazarus back to life after death. . . . Abraham then bent over and gave Lazarus a big "welcome home" hug.

The angels then flitted and flew over to the rich man . . . and looked down upon him with disgust, . . . disdain, . . . and disease. . . . They whistled for some help, . . . and their devilish second cousins named Fire and Brimstone leaped onstage with a wicked laugh, . . . followed by a low-pitched moan, . . . and several a-cappella yelps. . . . Fire and Brimstone immediately spied the rich man and began tickling his neck and teasing his hair, . . . which brought the rich man back to life after death. Realizing that the rest of his eternal life would be spent this way, . . . the rich man looked up to see Lazarus smiling . . . and screaming . . . in ecstasy, . . . as he and Abraham watched their team win over and over again on Monday Night Football, . . . as the angels brought Lazarus and Abraham an endless supply of ice-cold lemonade, . . . which gave them both a dose of brain freeze. . . .

The rich man cried out to Lazarus in a voice like Elmer Fudd: . . .

Cue: Rich Man
[Speak like Elmer Fudd.]

Hey Abwaham and Lazawus, you wittle begga you.
Could you bwing me a big stwaw so I can sip some of your
    dwink?
I'm tewwibly hot down here
And these wascally devils awe weally bwinging me down,
    littwally.

Abraham stepped forward and spoke in a boring, monotone
voice: . . .

Cue: Abraham
[Speak slowly in a boring monotone.]

Well, well, Mr. Rich Man, aren't you in a pickle?
While on earth you ignored poor ol' Lazarus.
Now he's the only one who can help you. . . .
But he can't!
Because the gap is too wide,
And we haven't finished our unending supply of lemonade yet.

The rich man could only moan . . . and hiss . . . at this latest
news from heaven, . . . so the rich man called out to Abraham
one last time: . . .

Cue: Rich Man
[Speak like Elmer Fudd.]

Pwease, Fathaw Abwaham,
Could that wascally begga go and warn my evil bwother,
    Mudda, and Fadda?

Abraham, Lazarus, and the angels all had a good laugh at that one.
 . . . Then Abraham said: . . .

Cue: Abraham
[Speak slowly in a boring monotone.]

Ha, ha, ha.

Your family already has Moses and many prophets to heed,
     just like you did.

Ooops! But you didn't heed them, did you!?

My, bad.

And they are bad as well.

I guess ignoring the needs of those around you seems to run in
     your bloodline.

Oh, I gotta go, we're getting ready for the second-half kickoff.

And with that, Fire and Brimstone continued their attack on the rich man's hair and neck.

The end.

Props

☐ a Bible with the reading marked
☐ signs displaying the boldfaced subheads for the commentaries

Reading and Commentaries

1. Invite someone to proclaim Luke 16:19–31.

2. After the reading, present the following commentaries to the group. Before you discuss each point, hand the sign displaying its subhead to the skit character it best applies to, and have that person stand in front of the group as you walk everyone through the meaning of the story.

A Parable for the Pharisees to Chew On

To understand this parable, it's important to know why Jesus was telling it. All of chapter 16 in Luke's Gospel is devoted to Jesus teaching about the use and misuse of wealth. In the section immediately preceding this story (Luke 16:14–18), Jesus clearly challenges the Pharisees (religious leaders of his day) about their own misuse of wealth and power, especially as they apply the Law to others. In telling the parable of the rich man and Lazarus, Jesus speaks directly to the Pharisees, comparing them to the rich man, who does not seem to notice the eternal consequences to which his misuse of wealth leads him.

Richer than Rich

Luke's parable paints an image of a man so rich that even the food he wastes would be considered a special treat by most of the working class. The fine purple garments and linens (verse 19) he wears were extremely expensive and only worn by the wealthiest of that day. Clearly the rich man had more than his share of wealth, food, clothing, and material possessions. In fact, he had enough to share and still maintain a high level of living, yet he chose to focus only on himself and his own needs.

Poorer than Poor

Lazarus, a name which means "God is my help," is the exact opposite of the rich man. He is a sore-infested beggar who is totally defenseless and dependent on others to survive, so much so that he cannot even keep the street dogs away from him. He waits by the rich man's gate just hoping to be noticed and thrown some of the leftovers that fall to the ground, such as the pieces of bread that wealthy people would use as napkins to wipe their hands and mouths with and then toss on the floor for the dogs to eat. But he and his needs are ignored by the rich man, with no interaction at all occurring between them.

An Eternal Reverse

When death comes, as it does for all of us, the tables are turned. Lazarus gets carried away by the angels and placed in the highest place of honor, on the lap of Abraham, who was regarded as the father of the Jews. The rich man is buried and ends up in Hades, which was understood at the time as a netherworld that existed between heaven and hell. Here the rich man finds himself on the outside looking in, just as Lazarus had done during his life on earth. The fact that the rich man can see Lazarus and Abraham together only increases his own torment.

A Change of Heart?

All of a sudden, the rich man appears to know Lazarus's name and calls out to him for help. This is remarkable because he never seemed to notice Lazarus while on earth, much less address him by name. But it is too late for action now. Consequences have already taken over. So for the first time, the rich man begins to show some concern for others and begs Abraham to send someone to warn his family on earth. But Abraham refuses, saying that if they are not listening now to the word of the prophets found in the Scriptures and resounding through the temples, then nothing will penetrate their lives of comfort and their hardened hearts.

Action Not Words

In the end, the rich man spends all eternity waiting at the door, looking in, just out of reach of paradise. What a terrible place to be—so close, yet so far away. Yet it was the inaction of the rich man while on earth that created this prison after death. Jesus reminds us that all we need to know to change that outcome is here before us, contained in our Scriptures, our traditions, and our teachings. But these remain mere words until we choose to embrace and act on them. It is the action, the reaching beyond ourselves, that will lead us to living the word of God in the world today, and that will lead us to eternal joy tomorrow.

(The commentary notes are based on Robert Karris, editor, *The Collegeville Bible Commentary: New Testament,* page 996, and William Barclay, *Barclay's Daily Bible Study Series.)*

Props

☐ newsprint
☐ markers, one for each participant

Reflection and Discussion

1. Explain to the group that the parable of the rich man and Lazarus is somewhat similar to what happens in Charles Dickens's *A Christmas Carol,* with the exception that Scrooge is warned and then visited by ghosts, giving him a second chance

to re-examine his life so that he can reorganize and reprioritize his values. Ask the participants:

- How might this parable turn out today if, in fact, Lazarus or the rich man were allowed to warn young people now?

2. Divide the participants into three small groups (try to keep the small group size to fewer than six). Give each group one sheet of newsprint and a few markers. Then assign one of the categories listed below to each group:

- a prophet from the past
- a prophet from the present
- a prophet from the future

3. Ask each group to develop a warning on their newsprint of what that particular "ghost" or prophetic voice might say to the young people of your community. If necessary, offer this example:

- The prophet from the future may come back to warn young people that their tendency to favor virtual relationships over interpersonal relationships has resulted in people of the future becoming more distant and disrespectful of others, with road rage and random violence at epidemic proportions while marriages and friendships easily crumble because people lack the skills to communicate face to face.

4. Offer the following questions to get each group started:

- *Prophet from the past.* Who and what are some of the voices from our history and tradition that have spoken to us about how we should live or use the resources we have been given? How might these past experiences be teaching young people today?
- *Prophet from the present.* Who and what are some of the voices that are speaking to us right now about how we should live or use the resources we have been given? What present "warning signs" or needs might be going unnoticed by young people today?
- *Prophet from the future.* Based on how young people are living now, what might some of the voices ten or twenty years in the future tell us? What scenes, images, or messages might a "ghost of the future" show us if this generation of young people chooses to ignore the needs of others?

5. Allow about 15 minutes for the groups to discuss and develop their statement. When they are done, invite each group, starting with the past, to proclaim its prophetic voice to the group.

1. Lead the group in a discussion of the following questions:
- Which voice—past, present, or future—is most encouraging? most troubling? Why?
- Who or what today is helping to proclaim these messages to us? How effective are these people or institutions in communicating these voices?
- What helps us to hear these voices more clearly? What distorts our hearing?
- Which voice is most challenging for you to hear right now? Why is this so?

2. After a couple of minutes of silence, invite the participants to think about a person, place, or group whose voice has helped him or her re-examine choices. Invite those who wish to do so to share aloud a prayer of thanksgiving by completing the following sentence:
- Thank you, Lord, for the voice of . . .

3. When all are done, close by inviting the participants to pray the Lord's Prayer together.

Acknowledgments

The information about Moses, Elijah, and Jeremiah on pages 23–25, 31–32, 39–40, and 48–49 is based on *The Collegeville Bible Commentary: Old Testament,* edited by Dianne Bergant (Collegeville, MN: The Liturgical Press, 1992), pages 83–92, 94–95, 308–309, and 454, respectively. Copyright © 1992 by the Order of Saint Benedict.

The commentary information on pages 57–59, 65–67, 76–77, 85–87, 93–94, and 103–105 are based on *The Collegeville Bible Commentary: New Testament,* edited by Robert J. Karris (Collegeville, MN: The Liturgical Press, 1992), pages 943–944, 969–970, 954–955, 995–998, 890, and 996, respectively. Copyright © 1992 by the Order of Saint Benedict.

The commentary information on pages 57–59, 65–67, 76–77, 85–87, 93–94, 103–105 is also based on *The Bible Library™ CD,* version 4, by Ellis Enterprises. Copyright © 1988, 2001 by Ellis Enterprises. *Barclay's Daily Bible Study Series* (New Testament), by William Barclay, revised edition. Copyright © 1975 by William Barclay. First published by the Saint Andrew Press, Edinburgh, Scotland. Also published by the Westminster Press, Philadelphia, PA.

During this book's preparation, all citations, facts, figures, names, addresses, telephone numbers, Internet URLs, and other pieces of information cited within were verified for accuracy. The authors and Saint Mary's Press staff have made every attempt to reference current and valid sources, but we cannot guarantee the content of any source, and we are not responsible for any changes that may have occurred since our verification. If you find an error in, or have a question or concern about, any of the information or sources listed within, please contact Saint Mary's Press.